Nearly Ca

THE TAMING OF PZ

A laboratory dog's search for love

Martha Ritter

Illustrations by Matt Ryan

This is a work of fiction. Names, characters, businesses, places, events, and incidents are either the products of the author's imagination or used in a fictitious manner. Any resemblance to actual persons or insects, living or dead, or actual events is purely coincidental.

First Hardcover Edition: February 2015

First Trade Paperback Edition: August 2014

ISBN 978-0-9863817-1-3

Published in the United States of America

by

Bradley Street Press
Stonington, Connecticut

info@BradleyStreetPress.com

Arrangements may be made for quantity discounts.

10 9 8 7 6 5 4 3 2

Publisher's Cataloging-in-Publication Data

Ritter, Martha.

The nearly calamitous taming of PZ / A laboratory dog's search for love by Martha Ritter; illustrations by Matt Ryan. -- First edition. -- Stonington, Connecticut : Bradley Street Press, c2014.

p. ; cm.

ISBN: 978-0-9863817-0-6 (Casebound)
ISBN: 978-0-9863817-1-3 (Paperback)
Audience: Ages 8-12.

Summary: When a mute, nameless foxhound gets rescued from her laboratory cage, a diva ladybug helps her understand the world and find a home with a restless, solitary girl. The dog and the girl must face their fear of connecting and learn to tame each other, let go, survive adventures, and find the courage to trust as they search for their place in the sun.--Publisher.

1. Dogs--Juvenile fiction. 2. Dogs as laboratory animals-- Juvenile fiction. 3. Dog rescue--Juvenile fiction. 4. Ladybugs--Juvenile fiction. 5. Trust--Juvenile fiction. 6. Human-animal relationships--Juvenile fiction. 7. Friendship--Juvenile fiction. 8. Attachment behavior--Juvenile fiction. 9. Grief--Juvenile fiction. 10. Self-realization--Juvenile fiction. 11. [Dogs--Fiction. 12. Dogs as laboratory animals--Fiction. 13. Dog rescue--Fiction. 14. Ladybugs--Fiction. 15. Trust--Fiction. 16. Human-animal relationships--Fiction. 17. Friendship--Fiction. 18. Grief--Fiction. 19. Self-realization--Fiction.] 20. Adventure stories. 21. Bildungsromans. I. Ryan, Matt. II. Title.

PZ7.R51495 N43 2014

[Fic]--dc23

Praise for
The Nearly Calamitous Taming of PZ

A charming, inspiring tale, carrying echoes of Charlotte's Web, *the book is immensely enhanced by its sweet and tender illustrations and humor. Ultimately, a well-told tale of a girl and a dog, each of whom grows in self-confidence and self-knowledge.* —**Goodreads**

Ritter is at her best when grappling with her main characters' internal lives, outlining in an accessible, realistically paced way how the psychology of grief and trauma can give way to hope and love.

Essential reading for anyone who has adopted, or is planning to adopt, a dog in need of love. —**Kirkus Reviews**

Thumbs up from a kid! Any person will feel good reading this book. I liked that I was able to get into the story quickly. The characters are unique, and bring funny and interesting spice to a good story about opening up and learning to trust. —**M. H.**

Authentic and sometimes hilarious. —**C. S. S.**

A book for all ages! I couldn't put it down. *I am 75 years old with tears rolling out of my eyes, and also laughing out loud. There is a wonderful way of writing that makes you feel every emotion an animal can have.* —**I. S.**

Lots of sensitivity and joy. —**C. W.**

Entertains and touches the heart—*much to ponder about the surprising twists in making connections. And a pleasure to meet such lively and beautifully drawn characters. A book for everyone!* —**M. K.**

Moving, authentic *portrait of a girl and a dog learning to trust.* —**R. D. C.**

I'm eight. I love this book! *I read it, then read it again and again because it is so good. It teaches you to try to be kind, to understand others, to see how they are feeling.* —L. C.

Magical! *The animals are so alive and believable.* —D. H.

A magnificently intelligent book. *I can't wait to read more from her!* —C. L.

Age-appropriate reading *for elementary school kids. The Taming of PZ is perfect!* —H. C.

I'm 98. A teacher for eons. Adore this entrancing, wacky book. *Kids get hooked, too, and soon you're discussing life's challenges, opportunities, and joys.* —M. G. S.

I highly recommend this book, particularly as a read-aloud family experience. —J. T.

Thumbs up from a children's librarian. —L. L.

I recommend this book for anyone and everyone. —A. S.

Not since Kafka has an insect risen to this level of artistic genius. —Dottie

A wealth of life lessons. *Part of the story—not heavy-handed or sentimental.* —M. M.

Ritter writes with the emotional honesty of a great fiction writer *and the piercing poetry of a seasoned journalist.* —R. M. H.

A delightful world where divas rule and second chances abound. *PZ and friends will get into your heart!* —Anon.

Profound and deeply touching. —M. M.

DEDICATION

To the students of Noah Webster MicroSociety Magnet School, apprentice citizens in our complicated world: may your wonder and curiosity explode into ever-expanding knowledge and an ability to trust and help the deserving people, creatures, and ideas that you encounter throughout your rich lives;

and to the memory of my parents, Patricia and George Ritter, two extraordinary individuals who changed the lives of many, from Connecticut to China. They had the same hopes for me that I have for Webster's children, who roam, as I did, the long corridors of squeaky, shiny wood connecting all those rooms of promise.

THE STORY BEHIND THE STORY

The story you are about to read grew out of the real-life drama of my foxhound, Tess, who lived in a laboratory cage as a breeder dog. Starting at six months old, her job was to produce puppies that would test medicines meant for humans.

When I adopted Tess, she was three years old. She knew nothing about the world outside of the laboratory. She didn't even know that there *was* a world. She was mute and nameless.

Experts said Tess was the most damaged dog they had ever seen. Most of them predicted that she would never connect with a human. She was so fearful that she wouldn't walk through a door to see what was on the other side.

When Tess finally began to venture out on short walks, people viewed her as a curiosity. She was a gorgeous hunter dog, but she never made a sound and sported a tattoo ID number in her ear. Children were especially intrigued by the silent creature trying to hide behind me. They had no idea how hard Tess was working just to look them in the eye.

By the time Tess was ten years old, she had become a startlingly kind and brave dog who *did* love humans. I wanted to write a book to answer all the questions about her challenges and her transformation. At Noah Webster MicroSociety Magnet School in Hartford, Connecticut, Tess and I shared my early manuscript.

We were regular visitors to Noah Webster for three years. I read the manuscript aloud, and Tess sat next to me, usually with her rear end facing the class—not because she was rude, but because she was shy. She loved going to school, and she collected lots of devoted fans.

We had great discussions about trust, love, fear, friendship, instinct, the cycle of life, the difficulty of being yourself, the wackiness of a fictional ladybug, poetic license, and, at one point, a pressing demand for potty humor. These themes resonated with adults as well, who happily plunged into the world of divas and second chances. A couple of years later, this book is finally complete.

When you turn the page, nonfiction will meet fiction, and you will arrive in the laboratory. Have a good read.

Martha Ritter
martha@tamingpz.com

Nearly Calamitous
THE ∨ TAMING OF
PZ

A laboratory dog's search for love

CHAPTER 1. THE LABORATORY

The foxhound was curled up with her pups nestled tight against her warm body. White with large, caramel-colored spots and long, elegant snouts, the litter looked just like their mother. The foxhound licked their backs as they napped.

She repositioned her hip to lessen the sting of the grated floor jamming her stomach. She stretched a leg until it hit the solid wall. Then she relaxed her neck and went back to work licking the pups. They were awake now, squirming as the grate pierced their own delicate skin.

Suddenly, the cage shook. The door flew open. A white towel in a big hand yanked a pup out and whisked it into the air. The little dog screeched as it landed in a smaller cage on a large double-decker cart. Then the towel grabbed the six remaining pups, one by one, until each was howling in its own cage on the cart.

The man wiped his forehead with the towel and rolled up the sleeves of his white lab jacket. "The kidney medicine arrived," he informed the pups. "That's your lunch! Hope you like it! You've got jobs now, just like your mom."

He slammed the door of their mother's cage, and the metal walls rattled. For a moment he looked into the foxhound's quizzical eyes, staring out through the bars covering the cage's rectangular opening.

"Time to say good-bye," he said. He strapped the puppies' cages to the cart. The mother foxhound looked away. "Your pups are as beautiful as you are. And they're stuck in this place, just like you." He shook his head. "You probably won't miss them chewing on you. But I bet those little guys are good company."

The man took a final glance to make sure that the pups' doors were latched. The walls of their new homes wouldn't be like their mother's. Except for the top part of her front door, the mother foxhound was surrounded by solid walls that were meant to contain the chaos of a family. But the pups' cages would have steel bars all around so the scientists could easily see any bad reactions to the kidney pills. If the pills didn't work for dogs, they wouldn't work for humans.

The man couldn't help himself. He stood for another moment and gazed at the confused little creatures about to start their life's work. Their big brown eyes darted all over.

He looked back at the opening of the mother's cage. The foxhound had disappeared.

But she was listening. This wasn't the first time she'd been through this. Nonetheless, she was never prepared. She was always snuggling with her litter when the towel came. She hated the screeches of the pups.

"I shouldn't have looked into your eyes," the man

whispered to her. "I won't be doing that again. You could break my heart."

The foxhound peered out of her cage. She didn't make a sound. She never made a sound. She'd become mute. That way no one yelled at her. Yelling hurt her ears and her feelings.

She'd taught her pups to be quiet, too, although right now that was impossible. She watched the man bump the cart down the aisle between the long rows of cages. She watched her puppies' reflections flash on the shiny metal cages and then vanish.

The foxhound's tail froze to its resting place on her belly, and she eased into the isolation that came between litters. Her long body dropped to the floor of the cage, and she exhaled. The grate dug into her paws and her stomach as usual, but she didn't think about it. She didn't think about how she never went anywhere, even for a walk.

She made the best of it. She knew the ropes. She'd been in the laboratory her entire life. For three years, she had nudged kibble and water from dispensers on the cage wall; she had peed and pooped through the grate onto her tray. She was just another of the thousands of animals who lived in the laboratory in cages piled one on the other. She listened to the monkey calls and pig squeals drifting in from unseen rooms. She listened to the yelps of her neighbors, all breeder dogs just like her. Their only job was to make puppies.

There were so many animals in the laboratory that it was impossible to name them all. They had numbers and letters for names. The foxhound was PZ-5934. It was tattooed on the inside of her right ear flap. A few minutes ago someone had flipped the flap again to see who she was.

More than anything, PZ-5934 wanted a real name. She'd learned to stop wanting anything else. She wanted to be like the big, hairy shrieking thing that got loose and swung from cage to cage through the room. The humans chased her and called, "Crazy Monkey! Crazy Monkey!" Crazy Monkey was not invisible, like the foxhound. She had a human sound, a name, attached to her. She would be remembered.

The foxhound stared at the dark walls of her cage, listened to her heartbeat, and licked her cuts. Then, for the millionth time, she stood and studied her view from the top row. Downward was concrete; straight ahead, an aisle separating rows of cages. On the wall was a clock. She liked the regularity of its ticking. She could rely on that clock.

She heard new pups in the cage next to hers.

"How many this time?" PZ-5934 asked her neighbor, whom she'd never seen.

"Eight."

"How are you doing?" asked the foxhound.

"I'm tired. My nipples hurt."

"Take care," said the foxhound softly.

Humans couldn't hear dog talk. They never heard the inside story.

She knew her neighbors inside and out. She knew which ones were good at being lonely, which ones couldn't handle it. She knew their scents. Through her cage's opening, she looked into the eyes staring out of other openings. Together they acknowledged their boredom, their emptiness beyond words.

All she knew was life inside. She had never been outside. She had no idea there was an outside.

Again, her cage door opened. Again, the white towel barged in. It grabbed the back of her neck. The hand dragged her from her shadows, hoisted her up, whisked her through the air, and slid her onto the cool examination table. She

stayed calm. She was used to it.

The people in white jackets looked down at her as they always did. They talked to each other, but not to her. With the politeness her mother had taught her, she let the humans finger her chest and stomach and peek into her mouth. She stood perfectly still. She held her paw up at just the right height for the blood-test needle to sink into her leg. Then the towel squeezed her neck again and whisked her back to her cage.

She landed on the dreaded grate. Her cuts hurt. PZ-5934 hurled her feelings into the shadows. She looked at the clock to keep calm.

At that very moment a laboratory worker across the room pointed at her cage and spoke words that would change everything.

"We don't need that one anymore," he said. "She's too old."

CHAPTER 2. OUTSIDE

The next day, a woman appeared at the foxhound's cage opening.

"I've come to rescue you, sweetheart," she said.

PZ-5934 looked out at the face. She had never looked into a human face before. This one was ruddy from years of caring for generations of dogs in the wind and sun. The foxhound knew nothing of these things. But she knew the woman was special. She watched her throw back her long gray braid.

The woman opened the cage door and reached in. She placed her hand on the foxhound's back. PZ-5934 had never been touched with something other than a towel or a needle. This hand was warm and gentle—shocking, really. Also shocking were the yellow and blue stripes on the woman's sleeve and the brown of her eyes—the only colors that to a dog's eyes were not gray.

The foxhound froze. She sensed the woman's generosity, but she shook off the hand just to be safe.

"You've brought enough pups into this world, my dear,

don't you think?" the woman asked lightly, taking the dog's cue and withdrawing her hand. "I'm sure you won't mind giving your job to a younger gal. You're coming with me."

PZ-5934 pressed her rear against the back of the cage. The woman didn't smell like anyone she had ever sniffed.

The woman put a chain with a leash around the dog's neck. The foxhound jerked back. She had never had anything around her neck. Surely, her head would pop off!

The woman tugged the leash gently. "Don't worry about the chain," she said. "That's how you'll learn to walk."

Where is the towel? wondered the foxhound. *I am going to fall!* Her insides shook. She shut her eyes and curled up tight.

But the woman put her arms under the dog's belly, lifted her out of the cage, and placed her on the floor.

PZ-5934 stared into space. The woman pulled on the leash again. The foxhound didn't budge.

"You are majestic," the woman whispered. "Your long legs are meant for running." She knelt and tried to look into the dog's eyes, but PZ-5934 looked down.

"Foxhounds chase foxes and rabbits and squirrels. You'll see. I am going to take you outside." She picked up the dog and carried her.

The warmth of the woman's arms soothed the foxhound. She rested her head on the woman's heart, as reliable as the clock.

The woman put the dog down in front of a door. The foxhound had no idea what it was. She shook so hard that she couldn't brace herself to sniff the crack beneath it. How could she know what was on the other side? A rumble in her stomach signaled vomit. She swallowed it back.

"Be brave!" coaxed the woman. "It's spring! It's a beautiful day! The world is waiting for you!"

PZ-5934 did not trust her. The big board in front of them had a knob. The woman put her hand on it, and the board opened!

The foxhound shook her head wildly as she tried to throw off the chain. Her legs flailed. She began to pant, her tongue a fluttering fish.

The woman lifted the dog over the threshold and placed her on the ground.

"You're out! Congratulations! Good girl!" she cheered. "It's okay. You're going to be okay."

The foxhound stood right beside the woman. New smells, hot and steamy, rose from the blacktop beneath her paws. There were no walls. Again, she shook.

The light made her squint. But still she could see a lot of big, shiny things, some resting in rows and some rolling past her. Above, little dark specks chirped and raced in the blue. Some got bigger and bigger as they zoomed downward. They were going to attack! Her tail dug into her belly. She turned and tried to dash back to the door.

The woman pulled the leash. "That isn't your home anymore." She guided the foxhound toward a van.

CHAPTER 3. A FRIEND

PZ-5934 wasn't used to walking, and the thing around her neck didn't help. She wobbled in a zigzag on the sidewalk. Suddenly, a loud, buzzing monster rushed straight at her. A man sat on the monster while it ate the shaggy ground. It was going to eat her! She jerked backward.

"Don't you worry! It's just a lawn mower! He's cutting the grass. If grass gets too tall you can't see where you're going. Relax. You're going to be fine."

PZ-5934 looked at the woman. Her mouth wasn't moving. Where had the voice come from? It was such a friendly voice. Rather fast but clear, and, amazingly, the foxhound could understand it.

The woman picked her up and carried her the rest of the way to the van. She placed her in a crate in the back.

The dog stopped paying attention to the lawn mower and the human. She had to know who was talking to her. She sniffed. She looked around. Her ears perked up. "Who are you? I can't see you. Please don't hurt me. I am new."

"Don't be afraid. Don't worry. I'd never pick on a helpless creature," said the voice. "You just need to get with the program. You're in the world now." *Maybe the voice is inside me,* the foxhound thought. *What is the world?*

The big thing the woman had put her in started to hum, and now it was moving! It was moving fast! She couldn't think anymore. She had to lie down.

There was a blanket in the crate. The dog's torn skin loved it. But she couldn't relax. The crate bounced as the van bumped along the road.

She squeezed her eyes closed. Then she opened them just a sliver. She looked out the window. Everything was new— big, floating white puffs up in the blue, and long brown sticks covered with crinkly things, which to her eyes were gray, but still astonishing. Even the air smelled different through the open windows.

"Gorgeous, isn't it? That's nature. It's mind-blowing, really," said the voice. "Sky, clouds, trees, leaves, all of it."

A little dot appeared on the window. The voice was coming from the dot!

"Don't you like nature?" it asked.

"Oh, yes, I do! But look at me. I can't stop shaking!" said the foxhound, holding up her jittery paw.

"You're scared silly!" diagnosed the dot, scrambling on the glass. "That's natural. It must be your first time outside, right? Go ahead and shake, or you'll get a headache. It'll die down."

To the foxhound's astonishment, the dot's back split straight down the middle. Then the dot rose into the air and jetted to a rung on the side of the crate. The foxhound

examined the tiny, shiny creature. "Yes, it's my first time out," the dog admitted. "Okay. I am going to keep shaking."

"Good. I know it must be shocking to see the whole world—including a little thing like me," sympathized the dot. "So, let me tell you. We're in a car. And the car is in the world. I live in the world, myself. I love it. Nature is the best part. You'll see. Most living things are born loving nature."

The foxhound kept moving her eyes between the dot and the world whizzing by.

"Am I a living thing?"

"Yes. You are a dog," the dot informed her.

"You mean *dog* is my name?!"

"No, silly. That's what you are. You're a foxhound kind of dog. I love hound dogs. I always wanted one. Laboratories love them, too, because you're so friendly—and you're the perfect size for a cage."

The dot flew onto the dog's snout. The foxhound studied its two minuscule eyes. Then she found that this odd-shaped animal had dots *on* it—two tiny ones on each side of its back and a big one in the center. Its legs were no bigger than hairs.

"Looks like our conversation is calming you down," the dot gloated. "You're not shaking anymore." Then it balanced on one leg, spun in a circle, and belted in a high-pitched voice:

Free at last
On the road
Forget the cage
Turn the page
Fill your...

"You *were* calming me," the foxhound interrupted as politely as possible.

"Don't mind me. I'm just celebrating. I've known a lot of caged animals, and trust me, it's good to be free. I'm happy for you!"

"I see. I have never met anyone like you before. I don't know if I'm happy or not. There's a lot to figure out. If I'm a foxhound, what are you? Are you a dot?"

"I am a ladybug."

"You are so teeny. But even you have a name!"

"Ladybug is not my name. Just like you're a dog, I'm a ladybug. I'm a kind of insect. And I'm a girl, just like you!" The dot flipped down to the next rung of the crate, closer to the foxhound.

"I'm a fine ladybug, don't you think? I am red, shiny, and fast! It's a pity I can't see red. And neither can you. But I hear it's beautiful."

"How do you know red is beautiful?"

"The butterflies tell me. They love their red! They fly like me. But they're bigger and have wings with gorgeous designs."

The foxhound tried to picture such a creature. "Will I meet one?"

"Oh, you will," assured the ladybug. "You'll meet hundreds of them. And I'll introduce you to another ladybug or two, if you're lucky," she teased.

"That would make me happy, I think."

"No doubt about it. Insects will thrill you. My mother laid a thousand eggs. Can you believe it? I don't think there are that many names in the world. Anyway, who has time to

15

name a thousand babies? So I don't have a name either."

"Oh, dear." The foxhound sighed. "You know, it's funny, but we're alike. No one named either one of us. Oh, I must think of a name for you."

The ladybug froze. "I can't even imagine it. That would be so wonderful. It has to look good in lights, though. I'm rather well known, you see. Take your time."

"I will. It has to be right. Well, you are red. I could call you Reddy. You're tiny. I could name you Tiny."

The ladybug didn't say anything.

The foxhound took that as a signal to keep going. *Hmm*, she thought. *The dot is round, the dot has wings, the dot has . . . dots.*

"I have it! I am going to call you Dottie—the dot with dots!"

"Oh!" shrieked the ladybug. She flew onto the foxhound's nose. "Now *that* is rockin'! I love the name Dottie! It's witty. It's charming. Good thing you didn't try to name me Spottie! I don't do cute." She shimmied around the dog's nostrils. "I have a name that puts me on the map! It's dancin' time." Her legs gyrated into a blur. "I have six legs, so I dance like a professional."

Water streamed from the foxhound's eyes. Her nose twitched. Her ears flapped. She held her breath. "Dottie, you're tickling me!" she said. "You have too many legs for my nose!"

The dog exploded with a gigantic sneeze, hurling the ladybug into the air. Dottie tumbled down the side of the crate but managed to grab onto the last rung.

"Yo! Careful there, foxhound. No more tornado sneezes!

I'm just a little insect."

"I didn't mean to sneeze. Are you okay?"

Dottie tested her wings and wiggled her legs. "I'm fine. Divas are made to last."

"That's good. What is a diva?"

"It's acting bigger than you are. And making sure everybody knows it."

"I thought that was called obnoxious," said the foxhound solemnly. "There's someone in the laboratory—I think she's a monkey—who's a diva. She gets loose all the time. She runs all over and screams. She thinks she should have her own room."

"Maybe she should," said Dottie. "She sounds like a monkey." The ladybug flew to the top of the foxhound's head, flipped over on her back, and waved her legs in the air in an upside-down moonwalk. "Maybe sometimes divas can get on your nerves, but it's good to have confidence. It's good to believe in yourself. And I don't act like a diva *all* the time. I can be very quiet and deadly serious." She flew to the window and stopped moving.

The foxhound noticed some strange drops coming out of the ladybug. They were yellow and stinky.

"Oh, Dottie! Dottie! Are you okay?"

"Of course!" Dottie scrambled out of the goo. "I'm just playing dead. That's my superpower. Doesn't it smell nasty? No one wants to eat me when I'm like that, trust me. No bird, no dragonfly. Forget it. To be honest, any ladybug can do that. But I play dead better than most, don't you think? I do it with style."

"You certainly do," said the foxhound, calmer now that

she knew Dottie was all right. "You sure have a lot of energy."

"Well, you would, too, if you had just napped all winter. Everyone should have the luxury of hibernation, I say."

"What's that?"

"I find a nice warm place and go to sleep in the fall. That's when it gets cold and snows. When I wake up, it's spring. The snow's gone. I guess if ladybugs stayed awake, we'd get lost in the snow. Yuck. This past winter I stayed in the laboratory. Your crate was the first ride out of town."

"You must have been at the laboratory a long time, then."

"Yes. A bunch of us found a great drawer near the oven in the kitchen. I slept behind a jar of garlic powder. Strange, I know. I guess it's a good thing I don't have a nose."

"If you're asleep while it snows in the winter, how do you know about snow?" asked the foxhound. She felt Dottie's legs exploring the inside of her ear flap.

"Once I met a horse who told me about snow," Dottie responded. "She was very smart, except that she let people ride on her back." She paused. "Oh, my, you have a number in here!" Dottie squealed. "A number and two letters, to be exact. Wow! A tattoo! Rockin'."

"Yes, I know."

"What's it for?"

"That's my name. But it's not a real name."

"You can say that again. PZ-5934," Dottie recited. "But it's better than nothing. I am going to rest in the circle of the nine, okay? It's perfect for me."

"Fine." The foxhound lay down, too. "You are so lucky to have a name. I have to get one. Even the monkey has a name."

"You'll get one. I know you will," Dottie assured her.

"Someday a human is going to love you and stay with you. And whoever that is will know your name and give it to you. You sure don't want to be called PZ-5934 all your life!"

"You're right," agreed the foxhound. "Why can't *you* give me a name?"

"Only humans can give a dog a name," Dottie informed her.

"Oh." The foxhound put her head down to contemplate this new information.

CHAPTER 4. A DEAL

The van stopped at a light. Dottie flew to the foxhound's snout and explained about humans.

"Humans and dogs have a special connection. You'll see. I'm not the right creature to be with you forever. I fly all over the place. That's how I found you. Ladybugs like to fly." Dottie slowed her words. "Plus, there's something else."

"What is it?" asked the foxhound.

Dottie's teeny eyes looked into the foxhound's. "I don't live as long as you do," she said solemnly.

The foxhound tried to take in the meaning. She sat up and looked closely at Dottie. "You mean I will be here longer than you?"

"Yes."

"I see."

"But don't worry. I'll be around awhile."

"That's good."

Dottie flew up to a luxurious, furry spot on the foxhound's head. She looked down the dog's long, sleek body.

"You look good. You just need to get some exercise. Of course, working out a little couldn't hurt. Then you'll be fast—fast enough to catch a bird. I'm not too keen on birds, just so you know. They're bigger than butterflies and can eat me!" Her pin-eyes widened. "I don't want to be impolite, but if you see one—or smell one—eat it!"

"Oh, my! I think I just saw birds over my head outside the laboratory," said the foxhound. "They're fast. How would I eat them?"

"You'll see."

"Okay. I will catch the birds so they won't eat you."

"Maybe you will," said Dottie. "Maybe you will." She crawled back down toward the foxhound's nose. "I won't tickle you. I just want to check out your great schnozzola!"

"My nose?"

"Yes." Dottie surveyed the foxhound's impressive nostrils more closely this time. "This is truly an enormous smelling machine. I wish I had a nose. I can smell a bit with my antennae, but not much." She flew up to the foxhound's eyes and displayed two thick threads. "Nothing like you."

"I see what you mean," said the foxhound, straining to see the antennae. "I could smell all the animals in the laboratory."

"Exactly. Maybe you should use your nose to find animals and then help humans chase them. I hear people sit on horses and chase foxes. Humans can't smell worth beans. I think it's your job to help them find the foxes."

"Really? That's amazing! That must be why I'm called a foxhound. But I've never met a fox. I don't know anything about them."

"I know." Dottie sighed. "There's a lot for you to learn."

She crawled from the nose along the dog's snout and stopped about halfway. "But when you see a fox, I bet you'll know it. I bet nature made foxes exciting for foxhounds. Why else would you want to look for them? When you find one, just make sure to tell a human so you can run after it together and have some fun."

"Okay. Thank you for being patient with me. You'd make a good mother, Dottie. Are you a mother?"

"No. It's hard to imagine having a thousand children. They'd cover your whole head. I wouldn't have time even to say hi to all of them, let alone teach them to tango. I dream of having just one child, so that one creature would be awesome. But nature doesn't work that way," Dottie said wistfully. "Are you a mother?"

"Yes. I've had thirty-two puppies."

"Wow! That's great. So you got to know them all?"

"Yes, for a while." The foxhound looked out the window at what was surely a bird gliding to a tree.

"It's almost the season when I'm supposed to lay my eggs," said Dottie. "I have to find a safe place."

The foxhound looked puzzled.

"You see, summer's coming. That's when nature likes ladybugs to lay their eggs. They're tiny, round homes to protect my children. It's quite a show. Each egg is bigger than I am. Can you believe it? And there are hundreds and hundreds of them. And I don't get fat."

"Nature is amazing!" The foxhound tried to picture eggs bigger than Dottie marching on for hours.

"Don't think about it," said Dottie. "You cannot always understand nature." She did some yoga stretches. "You know,

I have flitted here, flitted there, met all kinds of creatures, survived my dramas. But I don't know if I've ever done anything meaningful." She stopped stretching. "Maybe I'll stay with you instead of laying eggs! You are a sweet creature. You need someone to show you the world. Why don't I be *your* mother? Or let's say I'll be your friend. I will stay with you until you find your human."

"That sounds very good!" Being careful not to let Dottie fall, the foxhound bowed her head and closed her eyes. "I don't know how to live in this world. I want to do it right."

When the dog opened her eyes, they crossed as she tried to focus on the whisker where Dottie was now resting upside down. "What do friends do, exactly?"

"Friends help each other with the hard things in life," the ladybug explained.

"I never had a friend," said the foxhound. "I never had anybody. I think I would like to be your friend."

"Oh, fantastic! It's a deal!" squealed Dottie. She flew to the window and boogied.

CHAPTER 5. EARS TO THE WIND

The van stopped. The front door opened.

"Go to the Nine!" the foxhound yelled.

"I'm on it!" Dottie zoomed to the Nine on the dog's tattoo.

The woman opened the back of the van and unlatched the crate. Holding the leash tight, she lifted the foxhound out and placed her on the ground.

Everywhere the foxhound looked, she saw what Dottie called grass. It was clumpy and bumpy. Her legs buckled on it. A quiver rippled through her back. "There are no walls!" she cried.

"Take it easy! I see a fence! They must care about dogs here," Dottie told her, looking out of the ear flap. "And there's a gate."

"I don't know what those are!" exclaimed the foxhound, resisting the woman who was pulling on the leash.

"It means if you follow her, you'll be safe. A fence is a kind of wall."

"I'll try." The foxhound followed the woman through the

gate. They entered a meadow with a fence all around it.

"It's okay!" agreed the foxhound. "The fence makes the outside an inside."

"Right!" confirmed Dottie. "No surprises."

"You will probably never see anything like this again, sweetheart," said the woman. "A big field, all fenced in. Run your heart out!" She closed the gate behind her.

The dog looked across the meadow. How dazzling it was to be in the world, all that empty space waiting for her, the blue of the sky, the yellow of the dandelions, and the brown of the earth—all the colors her eyes could see. She licked droplets off the grass. "Delicious!" she proclaimed.

"Smell that earth!" Dottie called from the Nine.

The foxhound pressed her nose into the sweet, irresistible soil. Her superpower *was* in her schnozzola. The aromas wafting up her nostrils filled her with the company of other creatures. She could live with her face plastered there forever.

"You can probably smell every critter within miles!" the woman marveled.

The foxhound took in the scents of frogs and worms and snakes and raccoons and squirrels and rabbits and bats and skunks and, yes, *foxes*. She had no idea about their names, but she slipped easily into the web of kinship waiting in that meadow.

She could hear the earth: "Come, come, run! This is your home! I have been waiting for you! Be a foxhound!"

The woman removed the leash as though she, too, had heard the earth's call.

"It's time!" Dottie bellowed.

The foxhound's legs had been hibernating her whole life.

They stretched forward. They stretched downward. They started to walk. They buckled. Her cuts throbbed. She began to move. She picked up her pace. Before she knew it, she was running.

"You go, girl!" yelled Dottie, flying out from under the foxhound's ear. "I'm going to lunch."

There was no stopping the foxhound now. She galloped, her ears floating on the breeze, the sun warming her back. Her heart beat gloriously.

She did belong to the earth. Though she'd never touched it until now, the cool ground was oddly familiar. She ran along the edge of the giant meadow, past the shrubs where Dottie was hunting aphids. She sniffed and sniffed. She loved moving. Moving was surely something nature loved about itself.

Dottie watched her disappear into the distance.

At the end of the meadow, the foxhound saw her first flowers. They rubbed against her sides and tickled. She paused to sniff who'd peed there. A husky with a headache. A healthy dachshund puppy. She peed, announcing that PZ-5934 had arrived. Then, all at once, her legs collapsed. She thumped onto the earth.

She tried to get up, but her legs wouldn't cooperate. She didn't care. She was happy. Her blood pulsed. She lay in the sun. The damp earth eased the pain of her sores.

A delicious scent rose from the patch of spindly plants surrounding her. She closed her eyes and dozed for the first time without a bumpy grate beneath her.

When Dottie finished her lunch, she flew the length of the meadow. The dog wasn't moving. She tasted and smelled the foxhound with her antennae to make sure she was all right. She landed on a whisker and jumped for joy.

The foxhound's eyes snapped open. "Are you having a good time?"

Dottie hurled herself from one whisker to the next. "Yes! You have great trampolines! I can digest my aphids. I must have had a couple dozen. They're insects, too, even smaller than I am, but I eat them because they're wicked. They eat the food that humans want."

"Good." The foxhound took a big sniff of the spindly plants around her. "What are these? I love them."

"It's lavender," said Dottie. "It's divine. Nothing like a good nap in lavender and fresh air."

"My air always smelled like poop." The foxhound looked down at her exhausted legs. "I wish I could run again."

"Don't worry. Your legs will be fine. They're not used to moving. This will be quite an adjustment for you," Dottie said, landing near the dog's nose.

Together they looked out at the meadow.

"Yes, I have a lot to catch up on," said the foxhound. "Even your little legs are strong because you're used to going places. I like having you nearby."

"I like it, too," Dottie told her. "But I think it's time to go back to the human."

"Not yet! The earth feels so good, and I love the animal smells in my schnozzola." The foxhound stretched out her long body in the lavender.

"Actually, human beings are a kind of animal," said Dottie.

"They are? Are you sure? Are there ones with spots?"

"There are some with little spots. They're called freckles."

"Oh, my. So why is it that only a human can give me my name when I can't even understand what they say? Why not be named by an animal I can understand?"

"You'll see. You'll know when the person gives you your name. And you'll even start to understand that person. That's why you were rescued—so you can be a pet. We really need to go back."

The foxhound looked toward the woman, who was waiting patiently across the meadow. She tried to get up. Her legs were heavy and sore. But she was determined. She rose and began to trudge through the bumpy grass. Dottie rode on the dog's nose and majestically surveyed the expanse.

"What's a pet?" asked the foxhound.

"A pet is an animal that a human chooses to love and be with every day," Dottie told her. "Dogs are the experts on teaching humans to love."

"No way!" The foxhound laughed. "Have you ever been a pet?"

"No. But I have a brother who was. He lived at a school where they kept a ladybug colony. They named him Stan. He flew onto their noses and made them cross-eyed. The kids fed him raisins."

"Did Stan teach the children how to love?"

"I don't think so. Ladybugs are kind. But it's harder for them to show love than it is for dogs."

Dottie flew to the Nine as they approached the human.

The woman reached out her hand to pet the dog. "What a lovely time you had! That first run isn't easy. Your name should be Joy! I have never seen a dog run with such joy, you sweet thing."

She put the leash back on the foxhound. The dog jerked her head and wriggled in circles. They swerved and zigzagged back through the gate and up a hill until a long brick building stood before them. Loud barks and whines blasted out the windows. The foxhound sniffed.

"I think this is a shelter," Dottie said. "They take care of animals who have been rescued and don't have a home."

"I like the smells, but it's too noisy," declared the foxhound. "And I do not like walls that open. I will not go through that wall."

The woman pulled the leash. "We'll just get you inside."

The foxhound bowed her head and trembled.

"It's just a door," Dottie reminded her. "It won't hurt you. It won't make you disappear, or whatever you're afraid of. Doors protect you. There are doors everywhere. You'll get used to them."

The woman tugged on the leash again. Together she and the foxhound zigzagged a few steps. "This is going to be interesting," she remarked as she pulled four scrambling legs through the doorway.

CHAPTER 6. INSTINCT

The shelter was different from the laboratory. For each dog there was a large crate. In front of it was a small yard of fake grass enclosed by a white picket fence with a gate.

Each yard was separated from its neighbor's by another white fence with a big window above it at dog height. The window could be opened enough for a visit, but not enough for a jump.

The woman carried the foxhound to her own crate and blanket. She took off the leash and fastened a black collar with two tags around the dog's neck. The foxhound shook her head in an attempt to get the collar off.

"I'm sorry, cutie, but this tells the world where you live now," the woman said, fingering one of the tags. "And if you bite someone, the other tag says you had your rabies shot. Life is more complicated now."

She petted the dog gently on the head and then placed fresh water and dry food in the crate. "These are bowls. Check 'em out."

The woman held out a small morsel for the foxhound. The dog sniffed it. She liked the smell, but she didn't know how the morsel—let alone the bowls—fit in to her world. The woman put the morsel in her pocket and left.

The dog inspected the bowls. She crunched some kibble and lapped up some water. This sure was easier than using the tubes in the laboratory. But then she walked away. There was too much newness. She lay down in the crate.

Most of the dogs in the other crates were barking. And beyond, she heard and smelled other rooms of chaos.

Dottie crawled around the yard and ran her antennae over everything to get a feel for the setup. "I thought it would be more like a hotel. More privacy, a bit more luxury."

"I'm sorry you're disappointed," said the foxhound. "I am, too. I do not like this thing around my neck. And there is more barking than I'm used to. I think the dogs at the lab were too sad to bark all the time, and they had their puppies to watch out for."

"I don't like the sounds of these dogs," Dottie agreed. "They're obviously upset. Maybe their owners died or abandoned them or beat them. Who knows? But everyone's nervous. I can feel it."

Two women walked by. "I can't believe this is a rescue dog!" one exclaimed.

"Why, of course it is!" said the other. "They're all rescue dogs. This one's from a lab. You know how that goes—scared of her own shadow, not housebroken. Never seen a leash or stairs."

"But she's so pretty. She looks like a show dog!" said the first woman.

More shelter workers gathered in front of the foxhound's yard to get a good look.

"I hear she doesn't do doors at all," a man said. "This gal's got a long way to go before she's on the list."

The foxhound and Dottie didn't care that they couldn't understand. They were so tired that they stayed in the crate. Dottie hid in the curl of the foxhound's tail.

"I'm ready for my name," announced the foxhound.

"Well, I can guarantee it's not ready for you, foxhound. In this place, you'll have to earn it."

"Earn it?"

"If you're going to be a pet, you have to act like a pet."

"Oh, my."

"You have to do your business outside, you have to go through doors, and you have to feel less afraid."

"I will do it all! But it's been a long day. I need to sleep."

"Me, too," said Dottie, sinking into the dog's tail fur.

The foxhound fell asleep on the blanket. But early the next morning, she was awakened when the other dogs resumed their pandemonium.

The woman who had taken the foxhound from the laboratory appeared at the crate again. "You are so quiet," she said. "You could teach the others a thing or two." She put the leash and chain on the dog.

"Now there are *two* things around my neck!" the dog mumbled.

"Don't be afraid. I'm not going to hurt you." The woman pulled gently on the leash.

The foxhound shook violently. She backed into the corner of the crate and plastered her tail against her belly.

The ladybug had crawled into the dog's water bowl for a morning drink and had decided to take a swim. "At least I have a pool," she said as she glided effortlessly, her six legs synchronized.

"This woman is going to take me to another hole in the wall," groaned the foxhound.

"They're not holes in the wall! Those are plain old doors. Get that into your head," pleaded Dottie. "She will keep you safe, I'm sure. Now look at my backstroke. I have never done it in my life. My instinct is telling me what to do. It's saying, *This is good for you, and this is how you do it.* Isn't your instinct telling *you* the same thing about going with the woman? Smell her! Instinct runs the show!"

The foxhound continued to flick her head wildly. "I have to protect myself," she ranted. She studied the woman, who was peering into the crate and chanting something that was clearly an order.

"Dottie, where is my instinct? I just feel afraid."

"That *is* your instinct." The ladybug flew to the windowsill. "Instinct comes without your trying," she explained. "It tells you to run away from a lawn mower, or from a human you don't trust. Sometimes it tells you to be afraid. But you're afraid of everything right now, so I can see how you're confused. Just go with her, or they're going to kick you out of here. They'll think you're hopeless."

The woman pulled the leash again. "Come on, cutie," she said. "We have to go. We don't have trays here. You have to learn to pee outside."

"I can't go, Dottie!" The foxhound pressed every inch of herself against the back of the crate.

Dottie flew down to a paw. "I know you're scared. Bark! Buy some time."

"But I've never barked!"

"You have never barked?" Dottie was speechless for a moment. "Are you sure?"

"Maybe I barked a little when I was very, very new, but I don't remember it."

"Wow. But believe me: when you need to bark, you will bark."

The woman sighed and shook her head. She took the leash off the foxhound.

"Okay. Okay. Calm down. I'm going to wash your sores." She rose and went to her cart. She dipped a white towel in a bowl of warm liquid.

The foxhound saw the white towel coming toward her. She stood and braced herself for the woman's hands to grab her neck and yank her out of the crate. "Dottie, go to the Nine!" she cried.

"Oh, honey, it's okay." The woman bent down again and stroked the dog's head. "I'm just going to wash your old scrapes, you poor thing." She ran a wet towel over the foxhound's torn belly, legs, and paws. With another towel, she dabbed the dog dry. Then she squeezed some cream out of a tube and smoothed it over the cuts.

The dog let out a big sigh. She closed her eyes. The woman patted her and left.

The foxhound had never been without pain, and now it was easing. She was confused. If towels could do good, the world was turning upside down.

"If I may say something," came a deep, gruff voice. A dog

in the yard next door was beckoning across the fence. His head was at the open window. He was an old English bulldog with a wise-looking gray face.

"Who are you? Do you have a name?" asked the foxhound.

"Henry Ellsworth Bottsford the Third." The bulldog had an English accent.

"That's a beautiful name," the foxhound whispered to Dottie.

"What's your name?" asked the bulldog.

"I don't have a name. But I have numbers in my ear. You can call me PZ-5934."

"I say. Are you kidding?"

"No."

"Oh, well, what I want to say, PZ, is that I used to have instinct issues. I couldn't help overhearing your very interesting conversation." His voice was loud and pompous, but the foxhound listened politely.

"When I was a pup, I grew up with a cat," the bulldog continued. "She treated me like her baby kitten. So annoying. She did everything for me. I ignored my instinct to lick myself and keep myself clean because she cleaned me all the time. They say you're born with instinct, but it can get confused. You can pay too much attention to it, or not enough attention to it. It can be a frightful thing."

"He's full of himself," Dottie griped in a hushed voice as she sank out of sight into a crack between two of the foxhound's toes.

"He's my neighbor," the foxhound whispered back. Then she said to the bulldog, "I have never known a cat. I suppose that's an animal."

"Good grief! Yes. Dogs and cats are the most common animals there are!"

"That's interesting. So what happened to you after the cat made you into a baby?"

"The cat got old and died," reported the old dog. "But I have to say that after a while my instinct saved me. When I followed it, I found I was rather sensible and smart. It helped me to be safe. You see, instinct comes to you automatically like the sun or the rain."

"What are the sun and the rain?"

"Oh, I say, you are a strange animal indeed." The bulldog was baffled. "You are the most ignorant animal I have encountered in my life!"

The foxhound didn't know what to say. She didn't know what *ignorant* meant, but she could tell from the bulldog's scent and the tone of his voice that he was disgusted with her.

"*Ignorant* means you don't know anything," explained Dottie. "Don't listen to him. I am going to ignore him." She flew up to the Nine.

"What is a cat?" the foxhound asked Dottie.

"A little version of really big animals called lion and tiger. A lion and tiger will eat you. But don't worry, a cat won't. People love either cats or dogs. They don't usually love both."

"I see."

"The woman is back," warned Dottie. "I can see her shoes."

The woman stood before the crate. She bent down and put the leash on the foxhound once again.

"Let me tell you," Henry said, "this woman will give you a good education. She will take you to pee and poop out back.

She's gentle. And I like that sometimes she has a tail on her head. It's a tribute to our species."

"I have always peed and pooped inside in my crate," said the foxhound. She kicked the blanket. "But this is in the way."

"I say!" Henry blurted out. "I am shocked! We are all housebroken here! You must get with it, PZ!"

The foxhound looked at the bulldog quizzically.

"I know, *housebroken* is an insane word," Henry admitted. "It means you go away from the house, or away from the shelter, to pee and poop. You must become shelterbroken, I say!" He laughed. "That's part of being civilized, not to pee and poop inside. I daresay you are not quite civilized." He turned and started to walk away.

"This is my first morning in your world," the foxhound called to the bulldog. "I am inexperienced. And my vocabulary isn't very big. I guess instinct doesn't make you civilized."

"Don't listen to that old dog!" cried Dottie from the Nine. "Go with the woman. If you want a home, you must go with her."

"Am I civilized?"

"Well, you are polite, and you care about others. You're civilized in that way," Dottie answered thoughtfully. "But you don't know how the world works. So you're not civilized in that way. Don't worry! It will all come together. The woman is part of the solution. Please go, please!"

"Where do you pee and poop?" asked the foxhound, stalling.

"Oh, I shouldn't tell you this, but my waste is so tiny that I can leave it anywhere," Dottie boasted. "Most creatures only dream about invisible pee and poop!" she squealed, flipping cartwheels across the tattoo.

The dog studied the long, braided tail sprouting from the back of the woman's head. It was a wondrous thing.

"My instinct told me to study this woman! Well, I have done that. She smells okay. She was fine in the meadow. Maybe I have to have a conversation with my instinct the way Henry did."

"Good for you!" cheered Dottie. "I think that's what civilization is—a conversation with our instincts. But enough talking—just go!"

"Okay, okay." The foxhound put one foot in front of the other. She slid her side against the wall of the crate and stepped out into the unknown.

CHAPTER 7. BEHIND DOORS

The woman and the foxhound walked slowly down the hall. The dog dragged her side against the wall. When they reached the back door, the dog stood still. Her tongue fell out of her mouth, and drool dripped onto the floor as she began to pant.

The woman pulled the door open. She knelt next to the dog. "This is hard. I know. You will be okay, I promise you. You will survive. You won't get lost. You won't evaporate."

The music of the woman's kind voice lulled the foxhound. She sat and stared at the opening.

"I'll help you," said the woman. She quickly pulled the dog over the threshold onto a dirt path.

The foxhound was shocked. She was still alive. She took a deep breath. Her panting subsided.

"Well done! Bravo!" encouraged Dottie. "I'm going to breakfast. Ciao, bambina."

"What does that mean?"

"'Good-bye, baby' in Italian. A Sicilian llama taught me."

"Okay. Ciao, bambina," the foxhound repeated as Dottie flew off.

The foxhound smelled the ground and detected the urine of an old female German shepherd with a bad heart. She smelled a young male human who was unhappy. She loved sniffing the residue of creatures.

"Get busy. Get busy," said the woman as they strolled to a nearby tree.

Dripping pee here and there, the dog scattered her "hellos." Then she pooped.

"Good girl!" Hanging from the woman's fingers was the same delicious-smelling morsel that she'd offered the night before. Again, the foxhound was reluctant to deal with this foreign thing. The woman rubbed it gently along the dog's lips.

The foxhound licked the morsel. Then she opened her mouth and let it glide onto her tongue. It was delicious.

Dottie slipped unnoticed onto the Nine as they turned back toward the door.

"You look so bewildered, honey," the woman whispered. She picked up the foxhound and carried her through the doorway.

By the time the dog returned to the floor, fear was vibrating her whole body. Her eyes were dazed. In this place, who knew what could happen on the way through a door? Something might even eat her. If only she could tell what was coming.

"Oh, sweetie, don't shake," the woman said. "Doors are like a lot of scary things—they're mysterious only until you've seen enough of them. You either enter or exit. I'm going to show you a million of them until you wonder what all the fuss was about."

They started down the hall. Again, the foxhound dragged herself against the wall. They passed a door that had a strong human odor. *Now this is intriguing,* she thought.

The woman opened the door and turned on the light. Keeping her legs in the hall, the foxhound peered in. Dottie scrambled to the rim of the ear flap and looked in, too.

"A high sink and a low sink," the foxhound observed. She had seen sinks in the laboratory.

"The low one is a toilet," Dottie informed her. "For housebroken people."

"Interesting! Humans don't go outside to pee and poop? That's like me!"

"Foxhound, when you're not in a laboratory, your toilet is outside!" Dottie insisted.

"Okay. Okay." The dog lowered her nose and sniffed carefully across the threshold. She shook at the newness. But the smells were enchanting.

"Go for it!" cheered the woman.

The foxhound put one paw over the threshold and stopped, half in and half out. She stretched her neck and sniffed. Slowly, her back legs crept into the room.

The room was quiet and pleasant, but she still quivered. She eyed the giant water bowl that Dottie had called a toilet. She jumped up, secured her front paws on the rim, and plunged her head down to get a good drink.

"No! No! Honey, that's not for you!" The woman swiftly pulled the dog down. "Off!"

"I told you, that's for people!" Dottie repeated, peeking

out again. "For people to pee in!"

The foxhound bowed her head. "Instinct sure doesn't tell you everything," she said. "My instinct said, 'You're thirsty. You need a drink.'"

"You're right. Instinct doesn't tell you everything." Dottie flew onto the toilet's flusher handle and faced the mortified dog.

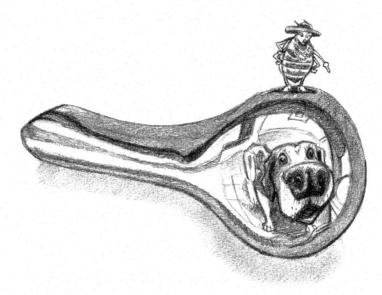

"Instinct will say you're thirsty, but it won't tell you not to drink from a toilet. Some things you just have to learn. And I guarantee you'll never forget a lesson learned from a mistake." She flew back to the Nine.

"I know what you mean," said the foxhound. "I will never put my mouth in a big water bowl again."

She stepped back over the threshold.

"Congratulations! You did it!" the woman gushed. "You went in, and you came out!" She held out a treat.

The foxhound ignored it. Everything in her was concentrating on being brave. She pressed her side against the wall and inched down the hall with the woman. She didn't like being afraid. She would never be a pet if she stayed afraid. With the woman beside her, she made herself walk right in front of a door with loud crashes coming from behind it, even though she was shaking.

"Good girl!" Dottie squealed. "You are awesome! Before long you will relish the world!"

The ladybug was committed to encouraging the foxhound, but in her heart she was worried. In a world with doors and toilets and endless mysteries to be discovered each day, who would take a shaking wreck of a dog?

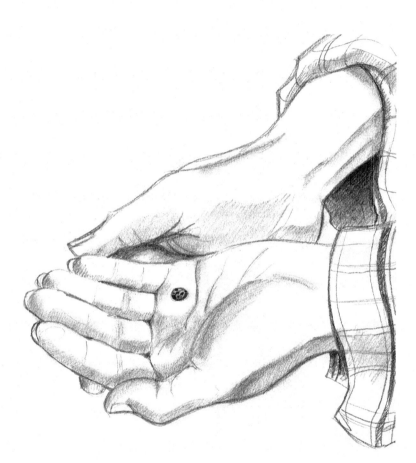

CHAPTER 8. AN UNEXPECTED MISSION

The woman returned the foxhound to her yard. "You walked by that noisy kitchen like a queen," she praised. "Good for you." She closed the gate and left.

Over the fence, Henry was lounging in his yard.

"Well, well, PZ, I see that you survived. Fancy that!" he bellowed toward the open window. "I bet you walked through a door, and here you are to tell the tale. No need to be a scaredy-cat anymore, my child."

"It is hard, Henry. I never had a door."

"Excuse me, but did you live under a rock?" Henry asked, his ancient, foggy marble eyes wide with shock.

"No. I lived in a laboratory."

"Oh, I say. I had no idea." Henry bowed his head. "I am sorry. I am so sorry." He paused for a moment to give respect to his neighbor. "I've seen one other laboratory dog. I should have known. She was as ignorant as you." The bulldog got up and walked to the window. "So I will tell you, the thing about doors is that usually there are marvelous things on the other side that are such a joy to inspect. On the other hand, some doors must be kept shut to keep us safe from dangers. Machinery that can cut you to pieces and such. We have to learn which is which."

Dottie flew to the windowsill in full view of the bulldog. "Don't make it sound so difficult, Henry Ellsworth Bottsford the Third!"

"And who are you?" asked Henry, alive with surprise. "Are you the tutor I hear chattering all the time? I have been wondering what you look like."

"Yes, I am the tutor. I am Dottie. I am a shelter insect."

"Oh, I say," Henry mumbled, dumbfounded.

"I am waiting to be placed in a home." Dottie fluttered her wings. "I, too, have had a hard life. The foxhound and I met in the laboratory. I'm a gardener."

"I say! What kind of home are you hoping for?" Henry poked his face through the opening to get a good look at Dottie.

"An insect-loving home." Dottie flew toward Henry's face and then made a U-turn back to the foxhound's bed.

"Good for you." Henry grinned at the thought. "I really like you girls. You have a lot of spirit, both of you. Of course, you, foxhound, are scared out of your wits, but I'm sure you'll be fine with the help of your little professor, I say."

Just then the woman arrived with fresh water and food bowls. "Oh, look, honey, there's a ladybug on your bed!" she exclaimed with clear delight. "Ladybugs are good luck, you know. We need to protect them. I'll just take her and put her outside."

Smiling at Dottie, she reached down, plucked up the

ladybug, and cupped her in her hands.

"Foxhound, follow me! Help me!" Dottie screamed as they started down the hall. "I am going to be executed! I just know it will be a savage death! Save me!"

"This is your moment, PZ!" hollered Henry. "Follow your professor! Be brave! The gate's not latched! Get out!"

"Oh, no! Oh, no!" cried the foxhound, trembling. Her legs marched out of the crate.

There was no time to hug the wall. She ran straight down the middle. Tracking the woman's scent, she came to a barely open door. She knocked it wide open with her snout and ran some more. A man walking a sheepdog tried to block her, but she was too fast. She reached another door. It was stuck. She banged it with her head and galloped through. There was no sign of the woman. A man with a poodle tried to grab her. She shook him off.

She smelled Dottie now. The ladybug had released her stinky goo. The woman was standing by an open door, the stink radiating from her hands. The sounds of the shiny things from yesterday were whizzing by outside. The woman lifted her hands to send Dottie out to join them.

The foxhound threw her head back. Her jaw opened wide. Every muscle in her body braced.

"A-OUUUUUU!" she howled.

She had never heard a howl like that before. It sounded professional. And it was her own! "A-OUUUUUU! A-OUUUUUU!" She jumped up and put her front paws on the woman.

"Holy bananas!" The woman gasped. "This is fabulous. I thought you were mute! You sing, honey, you sing!" Still holding Dottie, whose stink was strong now, she bent down. "Why are you so excited, sweet thing? You sure are a hunter dog! But you need to go back to your crate and be quiet. Someone will take you hunting someday, and then you can howl all you want."

She opened her hands to grab the dog, and Dottie escaped.

"Oh, good," said the woman. "She went out on her own. She's probably hungry after being cooped up. Wow! That's quite a smell." She wiped the goo off her hands with a tissue.

Dottie slipped unnoticed back to the Nine. "Oh, thank you, foxhound!" she exclaimed. "You howled! You saved me!" Swaying with emotion, Dottie rapped:

> *Ladybugs live a year or two*
> *That's a pretty good bet*
> *But believe you me, we insects need*
> *All the help we can get.*

"That's a beautiful song, Dottie," said the foxhound. "I'm glad I could save you. My instinct did everything!" She nearly skipped as the woman led her by the collar.

"That's how it works in a life-and-death situation. You don't have a conversation; you listen to your instinct." Dottie twirled on the Nine.

"You're getting frisky," said the woman as she guided the dog to her crate. "That's good . . . and bad. We'll have to watch you," she warned, and left.

Henry popped up in the window.

"I just howled," the foxhound announced.

"That was you? It sounded like someone was twisting your *toenails*."

"No. You were right. I had to get Dottie."

"Most impressive, PZ. Truly. So the little lady is still with us?"

"Yes. Can't you smell her?"

"Oh, my, I can. I say, foxhound! What a drama queen!"

"I can hear you," Dottie said weakly from the Nine. "Call me whatever you like. I cannot communicate just now. This has all been so upsetting. I almost lost my life. I was almost a rush-hour fatality. It's the windshields that get you. You can't see them coming, and then *splat*! I have a headache. I need to rest."

"I'll be still," the foxhound promised. She walked over to drink from her water bowl. Then she lay down.

"You recover, Dottie," Henry encouraged, also lying down to take the weight off his arthritic ankles. "Take care, both of you. It's good to have you on board. Not all newcomers show promise. And I think you two just might."

CHAPTER 9. A FRIENDSHIP GETS TESTED

The foxhound may have unleashed her first howl, but that didn't change everything. Her tail remained between her legs. She would need more experience if she were going to be a human's pet. Day after day, week after week, she spent the summer becoming familiar with the everyday objects of the world and trying to form new habits.

As the summer advanced, her days took on a more natural flow. She was comfortable in the collar and leash. She did her business automatically under the tree behind the building. She was accustomed to the ear-splitting barks of the other dogs.

The foxhound no longer dragged her body along the wall. She didn't quiver at the crash of a pot or the impatience of a person. She knew all the sounds and odors and personalities of the place—in the kitchen, the office, the laundry room, the grooming room, the closets. She even grew to like the feeling of rain coming down on her.

The foxhound started going up and down stairs. At first

it was an awkward and terrifying way to walk, particularly on the way down, and she had the uneven pace of a jumping frog, but she did it. And, of course, she still practiced going through doors.

Everyone at the shelter wanted to tag along and be part of the foxhound's progress. Everyone except Dottie.

"I am going to be direct with you, foxhound," she said. "I'm glad you're establishing habits, but I am getting bored out of my little insect mind."

"I'm sorry you're bored," the foxhound responded while practicing stairs on a sweltering afternoon. "I like habits. I need habits. They take away the mystery and scariness. When I go through a door now, I have more curiosity than panic. I thought you were curious about this place, too."

"Good grief! Not any longer. I'm afraid the novelty has worn off. I could write a catalogue from memory about the junk in their closets. I am sorry to say, but too much zigzagging gives me vertigo. I think I'll just hitch a ride on you to go out and eat, but that's about it."

"Fine, Dottie, fine." The foxhound was actually ready to spend less time with the ladybug. Dottie was a good teacher, but she was also one demanding diva.

Trying to make the best of hot afternoons with nothing much to do, they lounged in the yard. Henry helped with the conversation. "I say, we are so lucky to be in a no-kill shelter," he commented one day. He was perched at the window, his head on his paws.

"A what?" asked the foxhound.

"They don't kill you here, PZ."

"What is *kill*?"

"Heavens. You never cease to amaze me. You'd better find your tutor. I'm not explaining this one."

Dottie was practicing double flips on one of the foxhound's whiskers. She heard everything.

"I cannot explain everything to this dog, Henry." She paused to get her balance. "I am trying to do something for myself. I'm working on a trapeze act. It needs all my attention. The foxhound understands. I said I would stay with her, but I need more color in my life."

"Of course. I understand, Dottie," said the foxhound. She tried with all her might to stay still so the ladybug could perfect her moves.

Dottie flew off the whisker and landed on the crate. She ran all over it. "I thought I might find something. Yes! Yes! This will work!" she exclaimed. "I don't have to make a trapeze. There's one right here. Look!"

The ladybug hovered over two strings that hung from the ceiling of the crate. The strings, each a few inches long, were connected at the bottom by a stapled tag that said MADE IN WISCONSIN.

"This is more than I dreamed! Just push me with your schnozzola," she directed the foxhound.

"If that will make you happy." The foxhound complied. She thrust her head forward and propelled the strings gently with the tip of her nose. It made her cross-eyed.

Riding the swinging tag with great flair, Dottie assumed every possible position: her tiny head held high or bowed, her wings outspread or tucked in, on her belly or on her back. At all times, her legs were dancing. And she belted out her favorite song: "YMCA! YMCA!" Then she abruptly stopped singing to announce in desperation, "I really need a costume! Gold or silver. Shiny, to catch the light."

"Maybe when we have a home," the foxhound suggested. She was trying to be a good sport, but her neck hurt from the constant work of making the strings fly.

"Is it too much to ask for a cape?" Dottie went on. She hugged the staple with just two legs, soared to the top of the crate, and then rapidly descended. "I need a reward for staying in this place. Do you know who my ancestors were? They saved the orange groves and the lemon groves of California! They worked day and night to eat the little buggers killing those trees. And here am I, going insane in an animal shelter. It is shameful!"

"Your ancestors sound like great insects," the foxhound replied, exhausted. "I am sorry I didn't know them. And I am sorry you are so unhappy."

Dottie warbled nonstop. Her made-up lyrics annoyed the foxhound:

Stuck in a cage
Mind in a fog
All I've got is a freaked-out dog.

The foxhound couldn't take much more. She didn't know what to do. Plus, she had something on her mind.

"Dottie, please. I need to stop. I need to know what *no-kill* means. Please, tell me what it means. I know it's important. What kind of place is this?" The foxhound stopped pushing the strings.

"Okay. Okay. Let's take a break." The ladybug posed on the staple with her legs crossed like a movie star.

"A no-kill shelter is a good kind of shelter," she explained hurriedly as the trapeze died down.

"Good!"

"It means they won't kill you. Kill shelters put something in you with a needle, and then you're gone."

The foxhound jumped up. "Oh, Dottie, that's what I'm afraid of—that I will be gone!"

"I know. That's your door problem. Now, let's get back to practice. They'll never take me at the ladybug circus in Ohio if I can't do a double backflip."

"No!" snipped the foxhound. "I have more questions. There are other things I'm worried about. I need to know about—"

"Oh, foxhound, please!" Dottie cut in. "Think of me for a minute. How many questions have I answered? How much shaking have I witnessed? This is not exactly what I expected. I didn't know you knew nothing. *Nothing!* I thought I could teach you to love life. To love me. To find more joy after the meadow. I thought you'd be like a kite riding on the wind without a care. I thought each day would be a celebration after the laboratory. You'd be my best friend, and we'd have adventures in cool places, not in an animal shelter!"

Dottie's tiny eyes looked straight into the foxhound's. "But I was wrong. You are afraid to leave this place!"

The dog was stunned. "You said I had to learn to be a dog! You said you would teach me to be myself! I'm going as fast as I can! But you don't care about me. You just care about yourself!"

Dottie sat speechless on the trapeze. Then she dished it back. "Mark my words, foxhound, you are never going to be a real dog! You are going to be a shaking wreck wherever you go!"

The dog felt anger rising in her throat. This time she didn't swallow it. Her teeth grabbed the trapeze strings and ripped them off the crate.

Dottie tumbled through the air and crashed onto the floor.

The foxhound looked down. "Oh, no!" she wailed. "What have I done? Did I kill you?"

She nudged the ladybug with her nose. Dottie was motionless. The dog turned to the window. Henry was walking away.

She placed her nose so it just touched Dottie to let her know, if she were alive, that her friend was there. Then she waited.

CHAPTER 10. A GOOD SULK

The foxhound had no idea how much time passed. But finally she felt the slight flicker of Dottie's wings on her nose.

"You're alive! Oh, Dottie, how could I have done this to you?" She raised her head off the floor. "Oh, no! Look! Your trapeze is gone."

She studied Dottie. "Are you hurt?" she asked. Her tears fell onto the ladybug. "I'm crying! I have never cried before!"

"Yes, I'm hurt!" Dottie whispered, barely audible. "Now don't complicate it by drowning me!" She tried moving her wings. "One wing is dented," she moaned. "You can't see it. It's under my elytra."

"Under your red wing?"

"Yes!" Dottie caught her breath. She tested each leg. "Look, one of my legs is bent!" she cried in pain. "Look at it. I am going to be lame. Your ladybug is going to be lame!"

"How can I help you, Dottie?"

"Pick me up."

"How?"

"Try your tongue. Just lick me up and get me off this concrete. Put me on your paw. We don't need an ambulance or anything."

With great care, the foxhound picked Dottie up with her tongue and rolled her onto a front paw.

"Oh, I hurt! I am going to need therapy. And I am going to need rest."

"I'll take you to the water bowl. I will help you learn to fly again. Do you think you can fly?"

"I don't know," Dottie snapped. "We'll see." She looked up. "My, hound dog, you must have been really upset to do that."

"Yes. I was upset. I never showed anybody that before."

"You could have said, 'Dottie, you're driving me crazy.' Then we would have had a discussion."

"How can you have a discussion when you're going crazy?"

"It's possible. Look at me. I'm so angry with you right now. I don't even want to be here. Can you imagine if I injured your leg and you could never run properly again, maybe never run at all?"

"That would be terrible. I know."

Dottie pulled her injured wing in tight against her body. "This is very difficult."

The foxhound bowed her head. She looked at Dottie's tiny bent leg. Her tears fell onto the ladybug again. "I wouldn't blame you if you stopped being my friend," she said.

"I said, please don't drown me!" Dottie cried. "I'm going to need an umbrella!"

The dog shifted her head.

"Let's not talk to each other," said Dottie. "We need to sulk."

"What does that mean?"

"To be quietly annoyed." Dottie sighed.

"Okay, no talking," agreed the foxhound. "Only sulking. If you want some aphids, be on the Nine when the woman takes me out. But don't talk to me."

"Foxhound, I can't even get to the Nine! Dream on! Don't you understand? You have crippled me!"

"But the Nine is the only safe place!"

"What do you care if I'm safe?"

"I *do* care. Maybe dogs aren't good at sulking. If you get on my paw, I'll take you to my ear."

"Well, that's better than riding in your mouth where you'd slobber all over me!"

"Okay!" The foxhound lifted her paw to her head. The ladybug rolled onto it. Then she rode it down to the ear flap and flipped to the Nine.

"I really should be in the circus," she mumbled. "Fat chance now."

And so the dog and the insect remained together— the foxhound in her crate and Dottie recuperating on the Nine, the head spot, or the blanket—but they did not speak. Neither ate much. Mostly they slept and had occasional visits from the woman. After what seemed like years, but was the second morning, to be exact, the foxhound was the first to say something as they returned from a walk.

"Come on, Dottie, I'll take you to the water bowl," she said. "Do you think you can swim with five legs?"

From the darkness of the Nine, Dottie called back. Her voice was weak. "I don't know. I always use all six. That's what nature gave me."

"Spin to the edge, and I'll shake you into the bowl. I'll be very careful."

"I'm coming," whispered Dottie. "Be patient."

When she reached the rim of the ear flap, the foxhound leaned down and deposited her on the water.

"Oooooh, such a cool delight on a summer afternoon," Dottie gurgled, flipping onto her back. "To float and sip as though we're in Miami."

"I'm glad you like it. It's probably good for you."

"I think you're right. I have no pain in the water. It's magical." The ladybug floated like a little pea.

The foxhound put her head down near the water bowl. "I don't think dogs are good at being angry. I don't think I could go on if you weren't here."

"Well, a sulk can become a real burden," admitted Dottie. "But I did like it while it lasted. It was very satisfying. 'Nothing like a good sulk,' my mother used to say."

She looked up at the foxhound. "I will never, ever forget what happened," she said in her serious voice. "But I will not leave you. I forgive you. It is very hard because I am crippled for life and I hurt."

She dragged her legs through the water. "You saved my life. And now you've nearly killed me. Life is complicated. I used to dream that I could have you all to myself. Then I got sick of you. And now I have that dream again." She tried to swim to the foxhound.

The dog couldn't bear to watch her. "I won't leave you

either," she promised, looking away. "I'm sorry. I have never been out of control before." She turned back and watched Dottie do a slow crawl. "I will take care of you. I want to become a great dog."

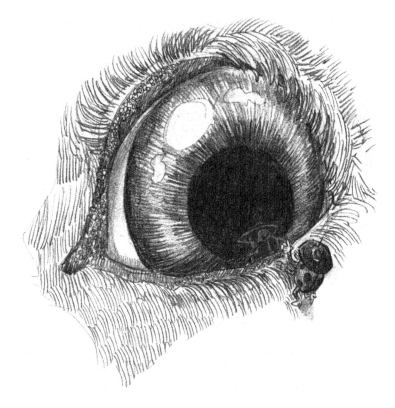

The ladybug looked up at the beautiful foxhound face hanging over her. "You will be somebody's loving, loyal dog," she predicted. "And that trapeze incident is one of the reasons why."

"Really?"

"Really." Dottie propelled herself the short distance to the foxhound's nose. Then she crept up to an eyeball. "You learned that you are capable of terrible things. It is just tragic that the terrible thing had to happen to me."

"Dottie, you are in my eye. Would you mind getting out? It is really bothering me."

"Of course. This was a very important moment, that's all." The ladybug hopped off the lower lid, turned around, and started inching toward the dog's ear flap.

"Foxhound, I really liked the way you told me to get off your eyeball."

"Thank you."

"If I may," came Henry's voice from the window. "I must say, I am glad the bug is all right. I was afraid the fall might have killed her. I had the misfortune of witnessing it. However, you have always lacked a certain assertiveness, in my opinion, foxhound, so in some strange way, this incident may be a sign of progress. With the howling, your door training, and now this trapeze incident, surely they'll let someone adopt you."

"But no one except us three knows about the trapeze," the foxhound pointed out.

"It doesn't matter. They'll see your confidence, your calm. Your skin problems have cleared up nicely, too, PZ," the old dog went on. "Plus, I'm sure there's been some improvement in the housebreaking department."

"What does *adopted* mean?" asked the foxhound.

"Getting your human," Henry replied. "I hope you find a good one."

CHAPTER 11. THE HUMAN CIRCUS

Henry was right. The people in the shelter marveled at the foxhound's progress. Something changed in her after the big fight. She understood her feelings better, and her confidence grew.

She was put on the list to go home with a human. Dottie could tell because the foxhound's woman scrubbed the crate and yard harder than ever. The white fence looked like new. The woman even removed the tangled trapeze and put it in her pocket. "I'm going to be sad when you leave," she told the foxhound, who was sitting on the grass with a look of bewilderment. "But you deserve a home. You've worked so hard."

Even Henry said he would miss his neighbor. "I'll give you one piece of advice," he offered at the window. "Watch out for children. They have so much energy, they will try to ride you like a horse. I don't have to worry, because no one ever picks me. No one wants an old dog."

"Thank you for the advice. I will miss you, too, Henry."

The foxhound walked over and put her nose through the open window. She touched the bulldog's nose. "Even though you called me ignorant, you encouraged me in your own way. I will never forget you."

"Good," said the old dog. "You were ignorant. And now you're not so ignorant. Those are facts, just facts, my dear. I will stay with you when the people come to look you over. It is stressful. You will be the only dog not barking, and by far the most attractive. And they'll see you are sweet. Everyone will want you."

"Oh, dear." The foxhound sighed, nestled into her blanket, and fell into a long nap.

She was rested when the crowd gathered a couple of days later on Saturday morning. The humans roamed around and studied the animals.

She sat high and straight like royalty outside her crate, her front legs stretched in front of her like two sticks. She did indeed attract more people than any other dog.

Dottie was at the edge of the ear flap, and Henry was in his yard.

"Pretend you're not here with all these maniacs!" called Henry. "Pretend you're in a sunny field!"

"There will be a perfect person! There will be!" called Dottie.

"I want that one!" a boy shouted to his mother as he pointed to the foxhound.

"No, she's mine! She is so cute! I have to have her!" cried a girl, trying to hurl herself over the fence to touch the dog.

Adults wanted her, too.

"Charlie, that one I won't mind on the couch. She keeps

herself clean," claimed a woman.

"Virginia, she doesn't bark, so we can watch TV," cheered a man.

People formed a long line to get a close look. The foxhound could smell the bacon and eggs, the burned toast, the coffee, the orange juice, and the Pop Tarts that the people had just had for breakfast. Their hands reached out desperately to land on her body. It was too much. She trembled. Their shrill sounds made her hair stand up. If they took her home, they would squeeze her and never leave her alone.

"I will run away if these are my people!" vowed the dog. She stood, turned toward her crate, and pointed her rear end toward the humans.

"This is a zoo!" shouted Henry.

"I was hoping for someone quiet," said the foxhound, still shaking.

"I was, too!" cried Dottie. "Quiet but fun. And respectful. This is an abomination!"

Henry shook his head. "There is something to be said for shelters, PZ."

The shelter woman worked her way through the throng. She faced them and announced, "This dog is unavailable."

Everyone stopped talking.

"Please move along," she requested firmly. "There are plenty of other dogs. There's a nice, obedient English bulldog here. He'd make a fantastic pet."

The foxhound had no clue what the woman had said, but she knew she was being protected.

"That's not fair! She's on the list!" the humans shouted.

"But I love her!" wailed a child.

"I can't live without her!" cried another.

The woman led the foxhound to her crate. "There has been a change of plans," she informed the crowd.

The people finally drifted away, and the woman sat down next to the dog. "You can stop shaking, honey. We will introduce you to some special people. People who will appreciate you. These were not the right people."

She held her hand on the dog's back until she was still. And then she left.

The foxhound curled up in her crate. "That was ridiculous. I'm not going to teach them how to love! What happens if I go with someone wretched?" the foxhound wondered. "I guess I would run away."

"Exactly! Bravo!" cheered Henry. "But why take the risk? Stay here."

"Oh, phooey! Foxhound, don't listen to him," piped up Dottie. She somersaulted out onto the ear flap. "You have to take a risk; you have to trust someone. Then see where it goes. This is how it works: a dog trusts a human, and then the human loves the dog. Then the human trusts the dog, and the dog loves the human. It's a big circle. Now, take me to the windowsill, foxhound. This is important."

The foxhound picked up the ladybug with her paw and set her down in front of Henry.

"I grew to trust an elephant once," she told them. "Can you imagine? He could have stomped on me!"

Henry stared at Dottie with raised eyebrows. "Where did you meet an elephant?"

"We're not talking about my life story, Henry. We're talking about trust."

"All right, all right."

"Did the elephant love you?" asked the foxhound.

"That is a private matter!" hollered Dottie. She willed herself to fly, with pain, to the dog's snout.

She took a moment to collect herself. "Trust is what you and I have, foxhound. It feels good. We earned it. We are honest with each other, and we support each other. We are loyal friends."

"Yes, I am happy about it," the foxhound told her. "And I am happy that your wing is flying a bit. But what if I find a human I like, and the human doesn't trust me back?"

"If I may, that is precisely why this hotel is so superb!" said Henry. "No one bothers you. And you certainly don't have to worry about love." The bulldog broke into a rare smile.

"Yes. I'll stay with Henry," said the foxhound decisively.

Dottie was silent. She hobbled to the dog's nose and gathered her strength to address both dogs again. "I am very sorry you think no home can do better than a shelter, Henry," she said quietly. "And I am very sorry you want to stay here, foxhound. But no one can force you to trust anyone. You have to choose to trust," she stated dramatically, and plunked down on her belly.

The foxhound opened her eyes and sprang to all fours. "I am really scared."

"So be scared," Dottie said. "That's what I told you the day we met. You can't hide fear. It'll just give you a headache."

"But if I'm scared of humans, I'm not ready for one."

"Just remember that real courage is being afraid and still moving forward," Dottie told her. She shrugged her wings. "You'll be ready when you're ready."

"Which may be never," added Henry.

CHAPTER 12. WHO NEEDS PEOPLE, ANYWAY?

The days got harder and harder. The foxhound became a robot, taking in just enough food and water to keep alive. She started losing weight.

Henry, who had become even grumpier than usual while watching the foxhound get sadder and quieter, cleared his throat at the window. "I have something that may cheer you up, PZ," he said. "I must tell you, it is quite possible that dogs don't need humans at all."

"Really? That sounds great," said the foxhound.

"Yes, quite," Henry confirmed. "Historically, dogs were independent of humans, you know. It's quite interesting."

"Gracious," said Dottie with a sigh. "How many thousands of years ago are we talking, Henry?" She twirled onto her back and buried herself in the foxhound's head spot.

"Dogs lived in their own packs in the wilderness. It doesn't matter when it was," the bulldog went on. "But over time they became curious about humans. Dogs especially liked inspecting the humans' garbage outside at night. They ate it, loved it, and went back for more. That's how they got to know humans and decided to stay with them—by eating their garbage."

"That is interesting, Henry." The foxhound perked up. "Maybe we should have a dog pack like the old days. Forget the humans."

"That's what a shelter is, essentially: a dog pack," said the old dog, smacking his lips with satisfaction.

Dottie flipped upright and faced the bulldog. "History may be interesting, Henry, but it's so yesterday! The truth is that now real dogs and real people *are* dependent on each other!" She rolled her eyes. "It is very hard to go against this rule of nature!" she warned. "Surely you must have played with a human at some point. Have you ever had so much fun in your life?"

Henry gazed at the floor for a moment. "I have to admit there is nothing as joyous as playing with a human."

Dottie and the foxhound looked at the bulldog in disbelief.

"But they never have time!" Henry added.

"Well, our woman will find someone who has time for the foxhound!" proclaimed Dottie. "This dog deserves the best!" She looked down at the dog's thin body. "But this can't go on!" she scolded. "You are so skinny that I bump into your bones!"

"I am not hungry," insisted the foxhound, curled in a tight ball.

"You have lost your hunger for life!" Dottie declared. "You want a new future, but you don't want a new future."

"I am doomed," moaned the foxhound. "I will never find

a human who understands me. People want to squeeze me and chatter at me."

Dottie walked to the point on the foxhound's snout where she went at serious times. "You are not doomed," she said softly.

"How do you know?"

"Because the other shy animals are going to a special room now. A spider told me. The greyhound with a limp, the tiger cat without a tail, the Great Dane with that squeaky bark. The humans in that room have got to be special, I just know it."

"Really?"

"Yes, really."

"I guess I'm a special case," admitted the foxhound. Her eyes were enormous and bewildered. "I need someone kind and gentle, but I also need to be left alone. And I wouldn't like licking everyone and cuddling. But I still want someone to love me." She bowed her head.

"We're all messed up one way or another," consoled Dottie. "Look at me! Look at Henry! What's so wonderful about humans is that they're more messed up than we are."

"Hear! Hear!" cheered Henry.

"When you meet the next ones, just use your instinct, foxhound," Dottie continued. "If someone doesn't feel right, just look down or walk away. They'll get the hint. It's all up to you. I bet the woman will take you to the room if you start eating."

Dottie was one bossy, but persuasive, insect. The foxhound trotted over to her bowl and ate everything. In just a few days, she was eating enough to go with the woman to a special room. It was very quiet and had two couches facing each other in a corner. The woman sat on one of the couches. The foxhound sat stiffly beside her on the wooden floor. Her nails made tiny, jittery movements that sounded like rain.

A cheerful young man wearing silver running shoes strode in. He had a treat, which he put in front of the foxhound.

"I will take you for long walks," he said, kneeling next to the dog.

The man was kind, but he didn't smell like a person to go home with. He smelled like fresh asphalt. And he was too eager. The foxhound didn't acknowledge the treat. She turned away.

"It's not a match," said the man. He walked out.

An older woman with white cotton-candy hair and red lipstick entered. "I have some nice dogs for you to play with, dearie. We will be your family." Her fingers, which

had strange red stains on them, reached out to scratch the foxhound's snout.

This human's attention was too far away. She was as unfocused as her hair. And she smelled like a wet broom. The dog rose and walked to the other side of the room. She turned her rear end toward the visitor.

"I'll go look at that cutie-pie Chihuahua," the woman announced as she shuffled toward the door.

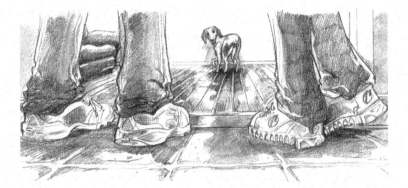

CHAPTER 13. OUT OF THE BLUE

Next, a girl and a woman came into the room. They didn't say a word. They walked to the couch.

The foxhound watched their every move. Her rear end still faced toward the couches, but she had turned her head to study the next contestants.

The woman looked calm. The foxhound could feel the girl's anxiety, though. The girl was biting her lip. She sat close to her mother and squeezed her hand.

Out of all the colors these people brought, the one most visible to the foxhound was the glowing blue of the girl's eyes. Those eyes told her something was wrong. They were sad.

The girl and the woman looked at the quivering, twisted dog with her tail between her legs.

The girl whispered in the woman's ear. The woman whispered back.

"What are they waiting for? Why don't they come to me like the others?" the foxhound asked Dottie, her ears twitching with anxiety.

Dottie strained to catch a glimpse of them. "They're being patient," she said. "But that is one nervous girl. They are probably waiting to see if she faints."

"I can understand if she's nervous," said the foxhound. "Look at *me*!"

"You two would make a fine pair!" Dottie said. "Really. Maybe you can help each other with your nerves. Can you at least turn around?"

Slowly, the foxhound rotated her body away from the wall and faced the new humans. She studied them. They still weren't doing anything. They weren't trying to make her do anything. They were just being themselves. It was the oddest thing. It wasn't complicated. She felt her tail move on her belly.

She stretched one paw toward them and sniffed. They smelled like the outside she loved, like fresh grass, like the man who'd cleaned her cage in the laboratory each day. Maybe they were safe.

She looked over at the shelter woman, who looked happy. Then she inched closer to the humans. She felt the generosity of the smile spreading across the woman's face. She sensed the woman's joy as her paws got closer and closer. But the girl hid her face in her mother's shoulder. She was trembling.

"Why is the girl shaking?" the foxhound asked Dottie.

"She's never seen you before," the ladybug explained. "She doesn't know if you're the right dog. You will spend years together. It's natural to be unsure."

"I can't stop shaking either!"

"It's natural. Just keep walking."

The foxhound kept going, her nails making the rain

sound on the floor.

When she reached the humans, she sat down in front of them. She looked into their eyes for one second and then quickly looked down. She liked these eyes. All four of them. They had room for her.

She licked the girl's knee. She wanted to calm the girl. She had never licked a human before. She was surprised that she liked the cool, salty taste.

Slowly, she lowered her snout onto the edge of the couch between the woman and the girl. She felt the warmth of their legs on her ears.

The woman ran her fingers ever so lightly on the top of the foxhound's head. Then, cautiously, the girl did the same.

"I like their fingers," the dog told Dottie.

"Stay with it, foxhound!" coached the ladybug.

The dog pressed her ear to the girl's leg and held it there.

"Hi," whispered the girl. She stepped down from the couch and sat on the floor carefully. She faced the foxhound.

Together they trembled.

The girl put her hands on either side of the dog's head and held it gently.

If ever the foxhound had trust, it was at that moment. Gazing sideways, she stayed in the girl's grasp.

"Lolly J.," the girl whispered. "That's your name. You are Lolly J."

The sound blew into the foxhound's ear, across Dottie, into the dog's brain, and down to her heart. That was the sound she'd been waiting for all her life. "Lolly J." The girl had said it with such special intention that it had to be her name.

The foxhound closed her eyes and let the sound

run through her.

The girl removed her hands.

The foxhound opened her eyes. The room felt different. She wasn't waiting any longer for someone to come. Someone

had come. She was now a pet sitting with her humans. She stopped trembling.

The girl put her hand on the dog's back. The girl stopped trembling.

"Lolly J.! Lolly J.!" chanted Dottie. There was no mistaking that specially delivered sound. "Now that's a name! We're going home!" She twirled on the Nine. "We're going home!"

The foxhound returned to her crate. She sat quietly and repeated her name. "Lolly J., Lolly J., Lolly J."

Dottie sang the name from the Nine. "Lolly J.! Lolly J.! It is the coolest name ever!"

That night the foxhound and the ladybug slept well. In the morning, it was time to say good-bye to Henry. The foxhound would miss him, even though she was sure his English accent was fake and he was a snob. He had encouraged her to be brave and to rescue Dottie. And he understood her difficulty in leaving.

The foxhound stood tall at the window, her long, muscular legs ready for new territory. They had gained strength from walking the halls. Her beauty and power now made it easy to imagine her as one of those joyful, carefree dogs frolicking near horses in a painting of a hunting expedition.

She looked over at the old bulldog, resting in his yard. "Henry, I think I'm going home."

"Oh, my, PZ, you're really going? I will surely miss you. I say, you have been one fine neighbor."

"You don't have to call me PZ anymore. I got my name. I finally got my name."

"I say, dear one, what, pray tell, is it? And who on earth gave it to you?" Henry pulled his old body up to await the answer.

"It's Lolly J. The girl gave it to me."

"What an odd name, if I do say so." The bulldog looked quizzically at Lolly J.

"Oh, dear. Is it strange? Is my name strange?" Lolly J. bowed her head.

"Well, my dear, most names don't come with an initial," he informed her. "The initial is usually an abbreviation of a name, the shortening of a name. Now, it looks as though you have an initial, but no name behind it. It is just odd, that's all I can say. What do you think you are, a rock star?" Henry laughed.

"Henry Ellsworth Bottsford the Third! You are in no position to make fun of someone's name!" Dottie scolded. She flapped her broken wing and forced herself to fly the short distance through the open window. She landed on Henry's nose.

"Can't you just wish her well on this day of all days? On this day that she goes home? There is a rumor that papers are being signed. It's official." She twirled her good legs on Henry's fur.

"I have told you not to tickle me like that," Henry reminded her.

"It's okay, Dottie," said Lolly J. "It's my name. And I will love it."

"Do you even know what a home is?" Henry asked quietly.

Lolly J. could hear the envy in his voice. "No. I have no idea what a home is."

"There are different kinds of homes," bellowed the bulldog, his eyes glistening with emotion. "You never know what you're going to get—maybe a mother and a father, maybe one mother, maybe one father, maybe two fathers, maybe two mothers, maybe some older people. Wait until you meet babies—human puppies." There was disgust in Henry's voice. "They make an unbearable racket and are totally helpless. They have to be waited on all the time. Anyway, all the creatures live together in a house or an apartment, like a giant crate. And trust me, those places are noisy. They have all kinds of machines that hurt your ears. The machine a man uses on his face drives me nuts. They have all kinds of rules that take years to understand. You're supposed to tell them when you need to pee."

"Really?" Lolly J. couldn't imagine it.

"They don't tell you exactly what you're supposed to say to get outside," Henry informed her, "and you don't speak their language anyway. So just wait. You will spend your life trying to tell them you need to pee, and it will take months for them to know that you aren't just dancing."

The bulldog shook his head as if to clear out the bad memories.

Again, Lolly J. bowed her head. Home sounded like torture.

"We are going home, Henry, no matter what you say," insisted Dottie. She managed the brief flight back to Lolly J.'s head spot. "Home, like anything, is what you make it. We will make it work."

CHAPTER 14. OLIVIA

That night, while Lolly J. sat in the shelter and recited her new name, Olivia—the girl who had given her the name—sat in the kitchen with her mother and refused to eat. She took what was left on her plate and scraped it into the compost bin.

"I made spaghetti," said Mrs. Palmer. "You said you'd eat spaghetti. I thought you were feeling good."

"Mom, I'm not hungry."

"But you were excited about the dog. I thought you fell for her." Her mother went over to the sink. "You lit up, Livie. You really did."

"I really tried. But I can't get those eyes out of my mind. She is way too lonely. I really saw it in those eyes."

Olivia filled a pitcher and watered the begonia on the windowsill. "I liked comforting the poor thing. I liked giving her a name. I was so excited I put the J. from Dad on Lolly. Lolly Jed. But now it seems like a bad idea. It's not a good combination. It's pathetic, actually. I don't want to fill the hole in her life. And I don't want her to fill the hole in my life." She carefully removed the brown leaves and dead blossoms from the plant.

"I need a dog to freak out when I come home and lick my face and run with me in the park. Freak out from excitement, I mean, not terror." Olivia held back tears.

"She's had a hard life, honey." Mrs. Palmer reached out and put her hands on her daughter's shoulders.

"Well, I've had a hard life, too!" Olivia squirmed out of her mother's reach. "My father is dead. I had him for ten years. How can I replace him with a dog?"

Mrs. Palmer shook her head and began to clear the table. "We're not replacing him. It's like his begonia. We're just keeping things going around here. We were going to get a dog with him. Now we're going to get one without him. It's been a year, Livie. It's time. And we all agreed we wanted a dog who needed us."

"I know. I know," Olivia said impatiently as she wiped up the water that streamed from the bottom of the planter. She looked at her reflection in the window: pale, oval face, black hair, blue eyes. She looked just like her father.

"We can't stay in our rooms and read for the rest of our lives," said her mother.

"Haven't you even noticed that I've started playing my violin again?" Olivia dropped her plate in the dishwasher.

"I know, Livie. Of course I know. I'm glad for that."

"And I'm trying to understand climate change, Mom.

That takes time," said Olivia. "And Grandma and Grandpa need me. The garden's over, but there are lots of leaves. And I need to take the stuff we canned to the basement. There's no time for this dog."

"It's great that you help them. It would be a good walk for Lolly J. someday, to join you," said Mrs. Palmer.

"We'll see." Olivia watched her mother, alone back at the table, lift her father's favorite coffee cup to her lips. "If Dad were here, Lolly J. would be like one of his clients. He'd know just what to do. I miss going to the hospital with him. I miss seeing him with all those sick people, telling him their stories. He knew how to deal with sad."

"I know," agreed Olivia's mother. "Maybe someday you'll be a social worker."

"Not likely."

"Well, who knows? You're so good with Grandma. She's not easy."

"I click with her," said Olivia. "I click with difficult people. I don't know why."

"Well, right now we have to deal with a difficult dog. And maybe you'll click with her."

Mrs. Palmer studied her daughter. "Livie, you are skin and bones! Don't you miss basketball?"

"I do. But how can I look at Dad's bench and see Mr. Robinson there?"

"Even if Dad were coaching, they wouldn't let you play. You've lost too much weight."

"I know, I know. Give me a break, Mom! I'm not hungry.

Quit nagging me." Olivia gathered her books from the counter.

"Watch your snarky tone of voice, Miss Palmer," warned her mother as she got up from the table and faced her daughter.

"Sorry, Mom. Just please give me a break with the food."

"Okay, okay, let's move on. You must have a hundred books on the floor. You've got to get a handle on your room before we pick up the dog. And we *are* picking up this dog. I told Lynn we're committed to at least trying. She brought her from the lab herself."

"Whatever." Olivia started toward the stairs.

Mrs. Palmer placed a book on her daughter's pile. "A little something I found in the library."

"See, isn't it nice to work in a library all day with books?" Olivia teased.

"It is, honey. But I have a life, too."

"No, you don't," Olivia snapped. "You're as bad as me."

Mrs. Palmer shook her head. "Who knows? Maybe you're right. But I'm looking forward to this dog." She picked up the library book and opened it. "'Foxhounds are strong, smart, and kind,'" she read. "'They love children. They love to play.'"

"Yeah, just like ours," muttered Olivia with a smirk.

"They're independent. They love to howl. They love to run," her mother continued.

"Just like ours," Olivia joked again.

"Well, this breed has a fascinating history. Let me see. 'They've been around for thousands of years, back to Egypt and Babylonia,'" Mrs. Palmer read. "'They've always helped humans hunt. They can follow a scent that's several days old across running water."

"Just like ours." This time Olivia laughed.

Her mother laughed, too. They laughed hard. Olivia had to put down her books and took a deep breath.

"Oh, dear, we'll just have to see how this pans out." Mrs. Palmer sighed.

"Yeah. Maybe we could observe the creature for science," cracked Olivia.

Balancing the foxhound book on her homework, she dashed upstairs.

CHAPTER 15. GOING HOME

M rs. Palmer picked up Olivia at school on Friday, and they headed for the shelter. Olivia couldn't sit still. "This could be a disaster," she said.

"Only if we let it be. The important thing is that we're going to try," her mother replied with determination.

"I'm going to think of this dog as an experiment," Olivia said. "Maybe I'll write a report: 'The Dog Who Had No Name Comes to Civilization.'"

"That would be interesting. Not many kids have this experience, I can tell you that," said Mrs. Palmer.

"Lucky them."

"My, you're spunky this morning," her mother observed.

There was no more opportunity for conversation. They'd arrived at the shelter. Lynn was waiting with Lolly J. out front. She had a big smile on her face.

The dog had had a bath. The white parts of her coat gleamed. Lolly J. leaned against Lynn's leg and looked up at Olivia and Mrs. Palmer as they approached. She wrinkled her forehead and started shaking.

"It's like she's in a washing machine," said Olivia, rolling her eyes, as Lynn led the dog to the wagon and lifted her onto a thick pink blanket inside the crate in back.

"This is a very big day for her, Livie," Mrs. Palmer said. "Try to be patient."

Lynn kissed Lolly J. on her head spot and then closed the hatch.

The dog's wide, pleading eyes stared out of the crate while Olivia and Mrs. Palmer got in up front.

"You'll be okay, honey!" Lynn shouted. She waved until the wagon disappeared.

Lolly J. and Dottie stared out the window at the trees just as they had on the way to the shelter in the spring. Now it was early fall. The leaves were starting to show their colors.

"I wonder what's with the girl," said Dottie. "She didn't even speak to us. I hope she's not a diva."

"I don't think so," said Lolly J. "She seems sad."

"We'll see." Dottie paced on the rim of Lolly J.'s ear flap. "I'm not sure how I'm going to introduce myself."

"You'll find a way, I'm sure." Lolly J. watched the homes whiz by and wondered which one would be theirs.

When the wagon turned into a driveway, they saw a brick house with black shutters. Dottie danced at the sight of it.

"Please don't tickle me when we get outside," implored Lolly J.

"Okay, okay. I'll do a slow dance."

Lolly J. glanced around the front yard as they drove up the driveway. "There aren't any shrubs!" she informed Dottie. "What about aphids? You can't live without aphids!"

Dottie looked out. "Oh, no, I am going to starve!" she wailed.

"Wait," said Lolly J. as they approached the garage at the back of the house. "There's a lot of holly! Just what you're used to! Aphids love holly, right?"

"Yes! Wow! An all-you-can-eat aphid buffet!" squealed Dottie. "Isn't nature smart? I will eat the aphids and they will keep me alive, so then I can do a service to our new community by eating more aphids and saving shrubs. I can do my job anywhere!"

"I'm happy for you," said Lolly J. "Now, go to the Nine."

"Don't worry. I know this is your moment."

Mrs. Palmer opened the hatch. She unlatched the crate, reached in, and wrapped her arms around the dog. "Hello, honey. Welcome to Clover Street."

Lolly J. glanced into the eyes of the girl, who was standing next to her mother, and quivered.

"There she goes," announced Olivia.

"What is this, some kind of welcoming ceremony?" Dottie muttered. "Let's get going. I want to see inside the house!"

"I know this is hard, Lolly J.," said Mrs. Palmer, trying to calm the dog by putting a hand on her back. "Livie, Grandma and Grandpa are probably in the kitchen by now. It's almost time to eat." Holding the leash tight, she lifted the dog out onto the driveway.

Lolly J. stood like a statue, staring into space.

"She looks like she's a million miles away, like she's not all here," grumbled Olivia. "She is beautiful, though, Mom, isn't she? I love her big paws."

"I love that little spot all by itself. It's so cute!" said Mrs.

Palmer. "A little island in the white. This dog is like an island, herself. Give her a hug, Livie, a light one. Let her know you're watching out for her."

Olivia bent down and held the jittery dog for a moment until Lolly J. slid free.

"This is going to take time. Lots of time," stressed her mother. "We'll get her a new collar tomorrow."

"And a name tag," added Olivia, "with my name on it."

"Yes. Now, remember, this dog has never been in a house before."

"I know. And she probably wants to pee." Olivia took the leash from her mother.

"Lynn said she's still not quite comfortable with a leash," Mrs. Palmer warned.

The dog zigzagged beside Olivia to the big tree in the backyard.

Henry was right, thought Lolly J. *It is hard to tell what people want when it comes to peeing.* The shelter woman had always said, "Get busy!" when they'd gone to the tree out back. But Lolly J. had peed there to answer the messages from the other dogs. Maybe she was always supposed to pee when she heard "Get busy!" So she peed when she heard those words from Olivia. But she also had to answer a great-smelling message left by a Labrador retriever so he'd know she was there.

The humans cheered, "Good girl!" Olivia gave Lolly J. a treat.

Just then Lynn walked up the driveway. "I didn't plan on coming right away," she told Mrs. Palmer, "but I had to see how she was doing. I miss her already." The two women looked over at Olivia and Lolly J. under the big red maple.

"Well, I'm glad you came. I think we're overwhelmed," said Mrs. Palmer.

"She'll start peeing on other dogs' marks," Lynn reassured her. "It's sort of like entering a conversation."

"We were just getting to that. I'm sure she'll find Ranger's scent. He lives two houses over."

"How's Olivia doing?" Lynn asked as they walked toward the tree.

"Between you and me, she's not too enthusiastic right now. But this could be so good for both of them."

"She is so nervous!" called Olivia. "She's doing her washing-machine thing. How long do you think that'll last?"

"It'll take some time for her to feel safe," Lynn told Olivia. "She doesn't like the leash. But you must keep her on it. Hounds are gone in a flash if they smell something enticing. It could be a mile away."

"Wow! Lolly J., you have quite a nose," Olivia commended as Lolly J. made her way along the holly behind the tree and dropped Dottie off for dinner.

"She's checking the perimeter like a little inspector," Lynn explained, "to make sure everything's okay. Instinct is so intriguing." She tossed her braid onto her back as she watched the dog zigzag onto the driveway. "I've been around thousands of dogs, and you want to know what I think?"

"Tell us what you think," said Mrs. Palmer eagerly.

"I think your Lolly J. is going to make it. Everyone will have to work at it. I think a dog who's been a mother can connect with people. Think of all the puppies she's connected with!"

"Puppies aren't people," Olivia pointed out.

The three humans walked with the dog toward the driveway as she shyly sniffed invisible finds.

"You're right, Livie," said Lynn. "Puppies aren't people. But she got to practice connecting with her puppies. She has to learn our rules now so she can socialize with us."

"I don't know if I ever learned to socialize. I'm not a very social animal," Olivia observed with an intensity not unlike Lolly J.'s.

Lynn chuckled.

"Well, at least I taught you the rules," said Mrs. Palmer. "We'll just cuddle this poor thing. She's been through so much."

Lynn stopped abruptly in front of the garage. "Caroline, this dog needs to learn to obey!" she exclaimed. "She needs order. Then she'll feel safe and trust people. If you just cuddle this dog, you'll ruin her."

"Well, I'm sorry if my instincts are off," apologized Mrs. Palmer, blushing.

"Didn't she learn some rules at the shelter?" asked Olivia.

Lynn laughed. "Oh, the shelter was more like, 'This is a bowl, this is a collar, this is a door.' Sure, she looks up to me because I've taught her some things, but I'm sort of a nursery school teacher, and now someone else can be the love of her life."

"Do you really think she could love somebody?" Olivia asked.

"Yes, yes, I do."

"It's so hard to imagine. She doesn't even know I'm here." Olivia pulled the leash to ease Lolly J.'s nose away from the wagon's exhaust pipe.

The dog went back to the shrubs in the yard to pick up Dottie. Olivia, her mother, and Lynn, continuing to trail the foxhound, did not notice when a certain insect flew into the dog's ear. Lolly J. then decided to stare at the light reflected in the side mirror of the wagon.

"She just stares," Olivia griped.

Lynn cleared her throat. "Do you know what this dog has been through, Livie?"

"Sort of."

"Well, if you imagine being locked up in prison, you'll get the picture. Actually, prison would have been better than the lab. At least she would have had exercise and some real human contact. At least she might have seen light coming in through a window."

"Are you kidding me?"

"Livie, she was all by herself in a shadowy cage. A couple of times a week she went to a slightly larger cage to take a couple of steps. That was her big workout. I'm not kidding. And no one talked to her. She was like a piece of meat."

"No way!" Olivia looked at Lolly J., who was still staring at the light in the mirror.

Lynn told Olivia and Mrs. Palmer about the solid walls, the small opening, and the grated floor.

"This is hard to hear," said Mrs. Palmer.

"It is," agreed Olivia. "She may be closed off forever."

Lolly J. stepped over to Lynn and stood next to her.

"She's so attached to you!" Olivia observed. "She'll hate me if I try to socialize her. It will be like trying to socialize a giraffe! Plus, I hate to say it, but who has time for this?" Olivia looked at her mother. "Mom, I'm just trying to be honest here in the beginning."

"There are different ways to solve problems," her mother said.

"Yes, I am the only person she knows," Lynn acknowledged. "And I will visit. But she's ready to get to know you, Livie. If you're not ready, I hate to say it, but this is not where this dog belongs. Or, certainly, your mother could be the main person in her life."

Lolly J.'s quivers shook the leash all the way up to Olivia's hand. "I appreciate the chance for this growth experience," Olivia said. "It just seems almost impossible." The dog leaned into Lynn's leg.

"I'll just tell you this," said Lynn. "It's my job to think about the welfare of this dog. I am also your friend, and I have told you that I truly believe she could be a lovely dog for you and your mom. You are both smart and caring." She stroked the foxhound's ear. "Dogs like to be in a pack. And they desperately want a pack leader. You and your mom and your grandparents would make a great pack. But one of you needs to be the master."

Lolly J. lay down. She sniffed Lynn's boot and then rested her head on it.

"You really think I could be her leader?" asked Olivia incredulously.

"It's up to you, Livie. I think you'd be a good leader for her," said Lynn. "She would blossom if you made her feel safe. She's not hopeless. She ran her heart out in a wonderful meadow that day we took her from the lab. She'd never been outside. She was just so, so happy. Her legs weren't very strong, but she was a happy girl."

"Wasn't she scared?"

"Yes! But she was so thankful for that open space. Of course, the fence helped, too." Lynn petted Lolly J.'s back, and the dog let out a long sigh.

Olivia, too, put her hand on the dog, who was peaceful now, snuggling next to the only leader she'd ever known.

Lolly J. turned away from Olivia.

"I'm afraid I have to go," Lynn said. "I have to pick up some puppies. Their mother was hit by a car last night. You two sort it out. One of you has to devote yourself to this dog, or she will need another home. I've got to know soon. We owe her the best chance."

Olivia looked at her mother, who silently awaited her daughter's response.

"Okay. That's fair," Olivia said.

Olivia's mother took her daughter's hand and squeezed it.

"Great," said Lynn. She knelt to say good-bye to Lolly J.

The dog stood to receive Lynn's expert touch. She loved that hand on her back. It was the hand of a companion, but also of authority. Then she watched her only human friend walk down the driveway and disappear.

CHAPTER 16. ENTERING THE HOUSE

"Who's your visitor, Livie?" came a man's voice from across the driveway. Mr. Macgill, who lived next door, was getting out of his car.

"This is my new dog, Lolly J. The *J* is for Dad," Olivia informed him. "Lolly's short for lollipop. It was a joke name at first, but then I kind of liked it. She's not used to it—or to us. But she just peed her first pee."

"Well, congratulations. May there be many more." Mr. Macgill studied the foxhound. "She is a beauty. I'll grant you that. And I like that *J.* Your dad sure loved dogs."

"Yes, he did. This is her first home," said Olivia. "We're not exactly sure how things are going to go."

The dog had not budged from the spot where Lynn had stood. She trembled with her nose to the ground.

"Oh, I see. Is she a wild dog?" asked Mr. Macgill.

"No. She worked in a medical laboratory."

"Is she a scientist?" joked Mr. Macgill, his pink cheeks wrinkling with laughter.

"Brian, this is serious," said Mrs. Palmer as she headed for the house. "She was a breeder dog. They kept her very busy having puppies. This is a big transition."

Mr. Macgill walked toward them along the path between their yards. "I'm sorry, Caroline. I was just messin' with Livie."

"I accept your apology, Brian," said Mrs. Palmer at the back door. "I have to make sure everything's ready for our party."

"Good luck!" said Mr. Macgill. "It's nice to see you out and about, young lady," he told Olivia.

"Thank you," Olivia responded. She and Lolly J. remained on Lynn's spot.

"Good heavens, your dog is so nervous, Livie. She's shaking all over," remarked Mr. Macgill. "She makes me nervous. What a pity. She's one fine-looking hunting dog. Now, a dog is supposed to be your best friend, have adventures with you. Can she walk on a leash?"

"No."

"Does she know commands?"

"No."

"Does she play?"

"I don't think so."

"Oh, dear. This is a pickle. But I have to say, I commend you, young lady, for taking on the challenge."

"I'm supposed to be her leader."

"Don't be disappointed if she doesn't want to be led," her neighbor warned.

"My mother thinks we should try."

"I think you should, too. You never know what'll happen when you work hard at something. Let me know if I can help."

Olivia thanked Mr. Macgill. Then she guided Lolly J. toward the back door.

Autumn was Olivia's favorite time of year. Her feet made that crinkling sound on the driveway past the wooden lamppost her father had made. She loved the aroma of her grandmother's cooking when she came to dinner. Today she was making Olivia's favorite meal in honor of Lolly J.'s homecoming. Olivia inhaled the scents of roast turkey, fried plantains, and sweet beans.

"Stay calm," Dottie whispered to the foxhound as the girl carried Lolly J. across the threshold.

Lolly J. managed her crooked walk down the back hall and into the kitchen.

"Whatever you do, stay calm!" repeated Dottie.

Lolly J. raised her nose and sniffed the turkey.

Olivia's grandmother, Mrs. Rosas, was standing at the stove. *"Ven aquí, bella!"* she called to Lolly J. "Come, beautiful! Oh, how beautiful you are!" She opened her arms.

"She's going to be a handful, Jessie," cautioned Olivia's grandfather, standing next to his wife. He had a warm, open face and white hair. "She's not used to being a dog. You can put your arms down. She won't be coming to you."

"What does she think she is, a cat?" asked Mrs. Rosas, disappointed but smiling as she swept back the strands of silver hair that had wilted around her face.

"No one ever paid attention to her, so she doesn't know what to do. She's like an animal you might find in the jungle," explained Mr. Rosas.

"How do you know all this?" asked Olivia.

"I was watching you out back."

"Well, we have a plan," boasted Mrs. Palmer.

"Sort of," Olivia chimed in, removing the leash.

"Oh, my! I cannot believe how beautiful this dog is!" Mrs. Rosas bent down to pet her. But the dog vanished. She ran into the dining room and jumped on the table.

The foxhound stood as still as the tall candlesticks beside her, her head held high. She was transfixed by a big, fragrant mound of roasted meat. She looked at her new family and for an instant held her paw up toward them. She waited for someone to put a needle in her leg. But the delicacy was too enticing. She lunged and thrust her nose deep into the neck opening.

"*Ay, dios mío!*" cried Mrs. Rosas, standing at the doorway. "She's attacking the turkey! Tell your dog to get down, Livie! Timoteo, get her down!"

"Get off the table, Lolly J.!" cried Dottie, taking in an aerial view of the feast.

Olivia, her mother, and her grandfather ran to the dog. Olivia grabbed the dog's collar, and Lolly J. tumbled off the table. Glass bowls of beans and rice tumbled with her and smashed on the floor. The turkey, stuck to Lolly J.'s snout, catapulted, too. The dog shook her head wildly.

"Hold on, Dottie! Hold on!"

"What are you doing? It's like the *Titanic* in here!"

"An animal is stuck to my schnozzola!"

"Oh, no!" cried Dottie.

"Don't you eat my bird! No! No! Go find a pigeon!" shouted Mrs. Rosas. "Tim, take the turkey off her nose!"

Mr. Rosas pulled at the dog's collar. "Enough! Off! Off!" he yelled. Lolly J.'s snout popped out. Again she dove, and this time she tore a big, juicy bite out of a breast.

"No! Have you no manners?" screamed Mrs. Rosas. She ran to get a broom and headed toward Lolly J.'s backside. She was tall and strong.

Olivia rescued Lolly J. from her grandmother's reach and tried to wipe the stuffing off the dog's head. But Lolly J. bolted to the next room. She bumped into Mr. Rosas and knocked him to the floor as she cleared the corner and leaped onto the long table in front of the living room couch. *I'm ready,* thought Lolly J. *Get the needle! Get the towel!*

"*Ay, dios mío!*" Mrs. Rosas cried again. "Are you okay, Tim? Are you okay?" She ran to her husband.

"I'm okay," he declared, holding his bottom. "Probably just a bruise." He sat up and gazed at the dog, who was standing motionless on the table and holding out her paw again.

"She is *loca!*" cried Mrs. Rosas. "Livie, you must return her!"

Dottie sprang from some earwax to see where the dog had landed. "No, Lolly J.! No more tables!" she shrieked. "Is this the only trick you know? This is getting old!"

"I'm sure they want me on a table," responded the foxhound. "I just don't know which one."

"That was in the laboratory, you crazy dog! They probably examined you on a table and took your blood! You can put your paw down. Your family won't be taking your blood! They won't be examining you! They don't want you on their tables. This is a civilized home. Instinct will never tell you that. I am telling you. Thank goodness I have been around and I know these things."

"Are you sure?"

"They're screaming. Listen to them."

"They do smell unhappy."

"Yes." Dottie sighed. "This is not good."

"This dog needs a home!" insisted Mrs. Palmer, helping her father off the floor.

"But we don't need her, darling, really," argued Mrs. Rosas, still clutching the broom. "We don't need this commotion. And this animal is dangerous."

"She has no one," Olivia reminded her grandmother as well as herself. "I guess she feels safe on tables away from us all."

Lolly J. jumped down. She sat in front of everyone, all

lined up now in the living room.

"Let's let her catch her breath," advised Mrs. Palmer. "She's checking out her new territory."

Lolly J. walked to the corner of the living room. Everyone watched as she stopped at a carved plant stand. On it was a small tree. She paused for a moment and then pooped neatly beneath it.

"No! No!" cried Mrs. Rosas. "That is not a toilet!" She ran to Lolly J. and nudged her with the broom.

"Grandma, please leave her alone!" Olivia pleaded, grabbing the broom handle. "She may be a pain, but she doesn't know any better. She found a tree. That's what she's used to."

"We cannot discipline a dog if we haven't taught her anything," Mrs. Palmer told her mother. "Please stop with the broom! We will put the dog on the leash, and Olivia will take her outside."

"We will live through this," vowed Mr. Rosas, limping with his granddaughter to the kitchen. He put the leash on Lolly J. and held the back door for Olivia to carry her out.

Mrs. Rosas took the broom back to the kitchen. "This animal is going to trouble us," she vowed.

"Well," said Mrs. Palmer, "it would be easier if dogs wore diapers and if they were born knowing everything about us. But it doesn't work that way. We're in for some adventures." She hugged her mother.

"*You're* in for adventures!" Mrs. Rosas corrected her. "You can leave me out of it." She placed some ice in a plastic bag and gave it to her husband.

Mr. Rosas sat down at the table and held the bag to his

back. "I can use some adventure! I will help Olivia tame this dog. I may be a civilian, but I know what this dog needs: military leadership!"

"Amen!" exclaimed Mrs. Rosas. "Ship her out!"

"Olivia and I will be her army," pledged Mr. Rosas.

Mrs. Rosas rolled her eyes.

"We'll see what happens," said Mrs. Palmer. "I'd better clean up the glass. Then I'll order a pizza."

CHAPTER 17. NIGHT AND DAY

As the commotion was dying down, Olivia held the leash while Lolly J. sniffed and peed in the backyard.

"Good girl!" said Olivia. She fished a treat out of her pocket.

The dog ignored the treat. Her head darted about rapidly in the dusky light as the humans' earlier shouts echoed in her head.

"Yikes, you look so bewildered—like you were just born or something," said Olivia. She put the treat back in her pocket, then hoisted the dog into her arms and carried her back inside.

Mr. Rosas suggested that Olivia keep the leash on. She and Lolly J. walked together into the living room to the palm tree, and she picked up the poop with a bag.

"This was not a good move," she said to Lolly J., who sniffed the location of her accident with great interest. "But how you're going to get the message, I have no clue. I'll take you to your crate."

Olivia led the dog to the bottom of the stairs.

"Now she wants me to walk up in the air!" Lolly J. was transfixed by the steps.

Dottie peered out. "You can do stairs! You practiced enough to walk to the moon on stairs! Don't think about it!"

"But I never did more than five steps at once. These go on forever. Okay. I'm no monkey, but I can do it." The dog flattened her side against the wall. She placed one paw on the first step next to Olivia's foot, and slowly they ascended side by side.

"Bravo! Bravo!" cheered Mr. Rosas, watching them climb.

"I bet you worked hard to learn that," said Olivia. "I can see you really do work hard." The dog was panting. Olivia petted her. Then they walked down the hall to Olivia's room.

Lolly J. stood at the threshold. She looked into the room. It felt enormous.

Olivia stepped in, and the dog stepped gingerly beside her. When Olivia removed the leash, Lolly J. ran to the crate, which Mr. Rosas had placed on the wall opposite the foot of the bed. She quickly curled herself into a ball on the pink blanket.

Olivia looked across the room at the frightened creature. "I'm sorry Grandma gave you such a hard time. You have a good rest." She closed the door and left.

The foxhound had always been in a room with other dogs. Their absence was strange. She'd never liked the barking, but she was used to it. A human home was odd. It seemed empty, and it smelled like not much happened there.

"You'll need time for things to feel right," Dottie reminded Lolly J. from the Nine.

Exhausted, they both dozed off.

When Olivia came back, she carried Lolly J. down the stairs and out the door for a last pee. Back upstairs, the girl stayed in the room this time. She lay on her bed.

Lolly J. watched her. She liked hearing the girl breathe. She liked Olivia's scent. It reminded her of the shelter meadow.

"I like the girl," Lolly J. told Dottie, who had decided to rest on Lolly J.'s paw. "But I miss the shelter woman. She knew how to talk to me."

"The woman was firm. I hope the girl learns to be firm," said Dottie.

"I hope so, too. I can't read the girl's mind. I thought I could poop inside."

"Did you poop inside?" asked Dottie. "How did I miss that?"

"You were on the Nine."

"I can't catch everything. I wondered why that woman screamed and the girl took you out so fast. I thought they'd had it with the tables. You know better than to poop inside, Lolly J."

"But I did it under a tree."

"It doesn't matter. No peeing and pooping inside even if there's a tree," Dottie recited wearily.

"Oh, dear. It's complicated. I do not know what is expected of me."

And so they lay in the silence of 232 Clover Street. The only sounds in Olivia's room were a small tree branch rubbing against the window, a clock ticking, and Olivia sleeping.

Lolly J. liked the familiar tick-tocks. She liked the girl's nose whistles and bedsheet rustles.

"I will always remember this night," said Dottie dreamily. "This is the beginning of a new era."

"I'm afraid to walk through their doors," Lolly J. confessed.

"You walked into the kitchen. You ran into all those rooms. And you walked right into this room. Don't be so hard on yourself."

"I walked into the kitchen because of the smell of that animal. I ran to the tables because I wanted to make them happy. Humans like dogs on tables. And I came in here because the girl did."

"Well, it's good to have a reason to go through a door. Let's take one day at a time, okay?" counseled Dottie, stretching out for a snooze.

In the morning, the ladybug crawled back to the Nine. "Ah, I had a delightful beauty sleep. I slept like a peanut."

"I'm tired," the dog told her. "I didn't close my eyes. I looked out the window. I watched it turn from dark to light. I've never seen that before. Every window I've ever seen was covered except for when we rode in the shiny thing."

"That is night and day," Dottie explained.

Olivia came across the room and crawled into the crate. She ran her fingers behind Lolly J.'s ears. "Time to go out," she announced. She put the leash on the dog and pulled it gently.

Lolly J.'s head twirled, and she shuddered. *Now what?* she thought.

"Calm down!" ordered Dottie. "I am going to get seasick again! Just go with the girl. I have to get outside. I'm starving. And you need to relieve yourself."

Olivia scratched the dog's tummy. "Come on. We're going

to the vet today."

Suddenly, the girl jerked backward. "Oh, no! Oh, no! Mommy, come quick!" she screamed. "Something's coming out of Lolly J.'s ear! It's yellow! It stinks! Oh, no!"

The nasty smell raced up Lolly J.'s nostrils. She knew that smell. "Are you crazy, Dottie? This is our first whole day at home. Why do you have to draw attention to yourself? Sometimes I wish you weren't a diva."

"I'm not showing off this time!" Dottie cried. "Honest! I must be as nervous as you are. It was an accident. I gooed." Lolly J. felt Dottie scurry around her ear.

"It's coming out like a faucet!" screamed the ladybug. "It's instinct protecting me from a predator!"

"Now you're making *me* seasick," snapped Lolly J. impatiently. "Why are you so nervous? The girl isn't going to eat you!"

"My instinct doesn't know that. She appeared too suddenly."

"Mommy, she's having an attack!" shouted Olivia. "Come quick!"

Lolly J.'s head darted back and forth. Her tongue dropped out of her mouth.

"Are you trying to throw me out?" yelled Dottie. "Stop!"

"No! No! Now instinct's got *me*!" cried Lolly J. "My head goes crazy when my ear itches. You're tickling me."

"I'm sorry," Dottie apologized. "I'll just sit on some wax and stay put."

"Good!"

Mrs. Palmer ran into the bedroom.

"Will she be okay?" asked Olivia. She slid out of the crate.

Mrs. Palmer bent down and stuck her head in next to Lolly J.'s. She inspected the substance on the dog's ear.

"She probably scratched herself. I'm sure she'll be fine. But obviously she's uncomfortable. I'll wipe her ear out. We'll ask the vet about it." Mrs. Palmer had a towel in her hand. She fingered Lolly J.'s ear flap.

"Dottie! Dottie!" Lolly J. screamed. "She's going to put a towel in my ear! She's going to squish you! Watch out! Oh, no!"

"Keep her occupied! Bite her!" ordered Dottie.

"What? Are you crazy?"

"Do you want me to die?" Dottie wailed. "I am too young to die in a glob of earwax!"

Lolly J. felt Dottie vanish from her ear flap.

"I'm down in the canyon! It's awful down here. You know I'm claustrophobic!" the ladybug shrieked.

Mrs. Palmer lifted the ear flap. "Goodness! You're right, Livie. It smells like something died in there!" She gave Lolly J.'s ear a quick wipe. Then the two humans left the room.

"What's she doing?" asked Dottie.

"They're gone," reported Lolly J.

"Good! I can't talk right now. I'm climbing the Rockies here. Remember, I'm lame."

"Take your time. I'll protect you."

"I'm sure you'll try, foxhound. I'm sure you will."

CHAPTER 18. THE FIRST WALK

Olivia returned to the room. "The smell's almost gone," she said to Lolly J. "Are you okay now? We need to go out." She coaxed the dog from the crate. Then they walked to the top of the stairs.

Lolly J. froze.

"Okay," said Olivia, "I'll carry you down one more time. But I can't keep waiting on you. It just won't work."

When they got to the back door, Olivia pulled Lolly J. through.

"Take your time, Livie. Let her explore," her mother called from the kitchen. "But stay close. I'll put the crate in the car so we'll be ready to go to the vet. Good luck!"

Olivia and Lolly J. stopped at the tree. The dog peed and then headed toward the edge of the yard.

"I'm going to do breakfast," said Dottie. "Pick me up later."

"Okay. Ciao, bambina!"

Olivia pulled the leash. "Let's go to the front yard."

Next to Olivia, Lolly J. zigzagged down the driveway,

which separated Mr. Macgill's front yard from theirs. She sniffed some messages. A rodent family and an old collie with a liver problem had been by. Then she stepped onto Mr. Macgill's grass to get a better sniff of the collie's mark. He may have been old, but he was a very happy dog. Lolly J. peed: "Hi."

"Good girl! Now get busy with some poop." Olivia tried to steer Lolly J. to the Palmers' front yard. She walked the dog halfway across the driveway, but Lolly J. refused to walk on the half bordering the Palmers' grass.

"Do you see a ghost? What is the problem?" asked Olivia. The dog wouldn't budge. "Okay, you win. Mr. Macgill won't mind if we walk on his lawn."

They'd taken only a step back onto Mr. Macgill's yard when the sound of a siren came out of nowhere. Lolly J. raced toward Mr. Macgill's front porch. Olivia sprinted at her side. The dog charged up the steps and leaped onto a pile of logs stacked in a large container by the front door. She wobbled on the unsteady wood for a second and then hopped off and squeezed herself into the tight space between the container and the house.

"No, Lolly J.!" cried Olivia. The siren, atop a police car, whizzed by. The dog's shudders rattled the logs.

"It's okay. It's okay," Olivia chanted in a soothing voice. With both hands, she tried to shove the container away from the house. It wouldn't move.

A truck rumbled past. A motorcycle blasted around the corner. Lolly J.'s shaking shook the logs even harder.

Olivia rang Mr. Macgill's bell.

He opened the door. "Good morning, Livie! What's up?"

Before she could answer, her neighbor caught sight of the leash snaking behind the woodpile. "Hmmm. Interesting."

"She's terrified," said Olivia.

"I guess so. I'm sure she's not very comfortable," commented Mr. Macgill.

"She probably feels safe, though," said Olivia.

"Yup. But we need to get her out, Livie. She has to face the world."

"It's her first day in civilization—her first full day."

"Well, it's understandable that she's frightened." Mr. Macgill shook his head. "It's just lamentable."

They hastily removed the logs and shifted the container away from the wall. Lolly J. sprang up on all fours in the expanded space, her eyes wide. Olivia pulled her toward the steps.

"Oh, my," said Mr. Macgill. "She looks as though her best friend just died. Not your typical foxhound."

"No," agreed Olivia. "Not your typical foxhound."

"I read last night that most foxhounds are particularly courageous," noted Mr. Macgill. As he threw the logs back into the container, Lolly J. crouched at each thud. "When they smell a fox, they howl like crazy and run thirty miles an hour. That's the speed of a car in town."

"I can't imagine," said Olivia.

"She does have a certain presence, though," observed Mr. Macgill. "A kind of mystery. A sweetness. Like she has more going for her than we know." He brushed chips of bark off his hands as he headed down the steps with a rake.

"Maybe you're right." Olivia carried the dog down the steps. "She may be special. But she's not normal." She placed

Lolly J. on the grass. "I've been reading, too." She tried to pet the dog's gyrating back. "George Washington brought foxhounds from England to raise on his farm. He was the father of our country and the father of our foxhounds. I like that."

"Yeah, I guess those early guys loved hound dogs," said Mr. Macgill.

"I don't get the hunting thing, though," Olivia said. "Wouldn't the howling make the fox run away?"

"I was wondering about that, too," said Mr. Macgill, carrying some lawn chairs out of the way. "It's kind of a game, I think. The fox knows he's being chased. He's fast and tricky, and he plays along. I guess he doesn't get caught much. It's sort of like hide-and-seek. When the hounds find the fox, I guess sometimes they all just play together like they've met up in a park."

"Weird!" Olivia chuckled. She helped Mr. Macgill move more chairs off the grass. She kept the leash wrapped around her wrist, and Lolly J. wandered behind.

"Did you read that you can't hunt a fox on a horse in England anymore?" Mr. Macgill asked. "It's against the law!"

"Are you kidding? I thought that's where it all started."

"Oh, the English will always love their fox hunting," Mr. Macgill stated. "But if you want to ride your horse and put on your fancy red coat nowadays, someone has to go ahead and drag a rag with fox urine all over the place to get the smell out there." He laughed.

"Double weird," said Olivia, giggling with her neighbor.

"I read that English hounds tend to kill more foxes than American ones do," Mr. Macgill said. "Maybe our hounds are friendlier, or not as well trained. Who knows?"

"I wonder if the hounds ever get to see a fox anymore."

"That's a good question, Livie."

"How do they get the fox urine and the scent?" Olivia wondered. "Wouldn't they have to catch a fox first? That would really be ironic."

"That's an excellent question, young lady," commended Mr. Macgill. "The world is getting more and more peculiar, if you ask me." He started to rake his yard.

"I'll look it up," said Olivia.

"Good. I know you're a good researcher. Keep me posted."

With rapt attention, Lolly J. watched the man pull the long stick and its feathery prongs through the earth and then push small, papery things into a big pile.

"Dottie! Dottie! What is that stick?"

There was no response. She had forgotten that Dottie was eating breakfast. She'd never experienced anything new without Dottie.

Mr. Macgill carefully repeated the same back-and-forth motion with the stick. Lolly J. kept her eyes on the movement.

"Of course, she's afraid of the rake." Olivia sighed.

"But I'm going to show her!" said a determined Mr. Macgill. "I am going to rake and rake until I have no grass, if I have to. Today she'll learn that a rake is not her enemy. That will be my first contribution to this dog's education."

"Great. I really appreciate it." Olivia kept Lolly J. close. "I'm sure you know how to teach dogs not to be afraid. You had a dalmatian in the firehouse, right?"

"We did, indeed! He died just before I retired. Louie."

"How do you teach them to be calm when there's a fire?

I hear they used to go to all the fires, but they never freaked out."

"Oh, you don't have to teach a dalmatian to be calm," corrected Mr. Macgill. "They're born that way. I just love those dogs. They quiet horses like a dream. In the olden days, when the horses had to pull the equipment to a fire, they'd get crazy. So the dalmatians ran beside them. They're like magic."

"Maybe Lolly J. needs a dalmatian."

"You be her dalmatian, Livie."

They watched the dog study the rake as Mr. Macgill made a large pile of leaves.

"I think she's less nervous now," he observed. "I think she knows the rake isn't going to attack her." He leaned down and stroked the dog's back.

Lolly J. didn't mind the man's hand on her. It was warm and had that treasured earth smell. But she smelled another scent, too. She pointed her nose up in the air and tried to locate the origin of it. She'd never sniffed a scent so intoxicating.

"All right!" Mr. Macgill cheered. "I'd say this dog looks happy to be alive!"

Oh, Dottie, I wish you were here! thought Lolly J., prancing near the leaves. *What is that smell? It is so wonderful!* She sniffed the man's leg to see if the irresistible odor came from him, but it did not. She moved away, put her nose to the ground to track the scent, and sniffed and snorted her way toward the leaves. *Oh, Dottie! Nature has something special for me, I know it.*

Lolly J. braced herself. Then, with the speed and destruction of a miniature tornado, she plowed through the leaves and scattered them high in the air.

Still holding the leash, Olivia plunged through the leaves, too. "Oh, Mr. Macgill!" she said. "We've ruined your pile!"

The man smiled. "Don't worry. I'm happy she's feeling good. Just think what courage it took to do that."

Lolly J. headed straight for the shrubs in front of Mr. Macgill's porch. Olivia loosened the leash, and the dog quickly disappeared into an opening. Smack in front of her, in a small clearing, was the animal with the fabulous scent. She sniffed and sniffed the thrilling odor.

CHAPTER 19. HUNTER GIRL

In the middle of the clearing, the spectacular creature stood motionless. Lolly J. cocked her head and studied the brown fur, the long, pointed ears, the nose twitching in terror. Panicked eyes stared into the distance behind the dog, as if they saw nothing.

Lolly J.'s heart quickened. She wanted to chase this animal. She couldn't contain herself. It had to be a fox! She was supposed to alert humans so they could chase it, too. That was a foxhound's job.

"Freeze! Don't move!" she ordered.

The creature remained as still as stone.

Lolly J. kept her eyes on the animal. Her tail shot upward. Her jaw dropped. "A-OUUUUUU!" she called.

The humans stopped talking. The foxhound let loose with another howl. "A-OUUUUUU!" She shook the leash.

"How amazing is that?" marveled Mr. Macgill. "I thought she was mute!"

"She was!" confirmed Olivia. "I can't believe it!"

Mr. Macgill and Olivia peered into the shadows of the shrubs. They could just make out the motionless, sandy-colored creature.

A few more howls erupted. The foxhound's legs were electric. She was ready to run with the humans—to run fast.

But the girl and the man backed away and resumed talking.

"So, now what?" asked the creature, daring to move its head so it faced the foxhound squarely.

"I thought we were going to chase you," Lolly J. said sheepishly.

The creature rolled its big eyes and exhaled with relief. Its ears relaxed. "Oh, my heavens! I thought you were a professional, the way you came in here. But I have never seen such an amateur hound. I should have known when I saw the leash."

"I'm sorry," apologized Lolly J. She bowed her head. "I will learn." She flashed her excited eyes up at the animal again. "But I am so happy to have met a fox."

"What? What did you say?" The astonished creature chortled. "Who are you? Where do you come from? I'm a rabbit!"

"Oh, my! I am so sorry!" Lolly J. said. "I don't know anything."

"That's okay. At least you got to practice. You can't practice enough for all the moves you need out here."

"I'm new here," Lolly J. explained.

"For sure, that's clear. I don't know what your story is, but it can't be good. Don't worry. You'll get the hang of it. Hunting is complicated. Don't hold your breath for a fox,

though. You'll find a lot more rabbits than foxes around here
... which is fine with me. A fox would have me for breakfast."
The rabbit's ears twitched at the thought of it.

"Oh," said Lolly J. "Well, I hope I see one fox in my life.
I have to see one, don't you think? I'm made to hunt foxes."

"Yes. I hope you find one. But remember, they're more clever than the rest of us are." The rabbit blinked twice. "I have to go now. After all your howls, I have to spread the word that I escaped a fearsome beast!"

The creature shrank into a ball of fur. "I can guarantee that you will never see a fox do this." It launched itself with its enormous rear feet, hopped high in the air through an opening in the shrubs, jigged its little white tail, and vanished.

Stunned, Lolly J. strode out to the yard.

"Look at your dog," said Mr. Macgill in wonder. "She explored! She sounded like a real hunter girl! She's going to come out of herself. I just know it."

"She did come out of herself!" said Olivia with a big grin. "Who cares if it happened with a bunny?"

Lolly J. was panting with exhilaration. For one moment, she lost her fear of what was coming next. She inhaled the rabbit scent deep inside her until it was a treasure.

"Come on, let's go home. That's enough socializing for now," Olivia said, still grinning.

Lolly J.'s tail snapped back to her tummy, and they zigzagged home.

CHAPTER 20. DR. FELDER'S OPINION

D r. Felder, the vet, wasn't as sure about Lolly J.'s future as Mr. Macgill was.

Mrs. Palmer had had to carry Lolly J. from the car into the building and then into the examination room. She placed the dog on the table, where Lolly J. shook and stared at the overhead light.

Dr. Felder stood next to the dog and observed her. He let her stay in her own world for a bit before touching her.

"She's in an extreme state of emotional shock," he said.

"What do you mean, exactly?" Olivia asked.

"Imagine if someone walked you through a door, and all of a sudden everything was totally different from what you were used to. *Everything*—what you see, what you smell, what you hear. You'd probably try to block it out, too. Basically, she's cut herself off. She feels threatened . . . by the unknown, I guess you'd say."

"But there's hope, right?"

"You know, Olivia, with animals you have to be realistic."

Dr. Felder's face looked wise and sympathetic. He had the patience of a man who had seen many sick dogs—even dead ones—and had helped their owners see what they had to see.

Olivia was trying her best not to cry. "I think I feel sorry for her."

"Well, I do, too, I can tell you that. No animal should have to live like this. But the fact is that she never had a normal life. She never had *any* life. She's terrified."

Ever so gently, Dr. Felder passed his hands over the reddish-brown swirls of the dog's long body. He examined her big, vacant eyes. "It would take enormous courage for her to stop protecting herself from us," he said. "She would have to trust that she'd be okay."

Lolly J. lifted her paw.

"Look at that," said Dr. Felder. "She's all ready for me. Dogs are such creatures of habit. Her habits come from the laboratory." He stuck a needle into her leg and drew blood.

"The man liked my paw up! I know it! He likes me on the table!" Lolly J. reported gleefully to Dottie, who had returned to the Nine after the dog's visit with the rabbit.

"Did he take your blood?" asked Dottie.

"Yes."

"Oh, my. I'll go to the ear canal just to be safe. He'll be in here any minute."

"She's calmer on a table," explained Mrs. Palmer. "Maybe she thinks she's supposed to be on a table. That's probably from the laboratory, too. So you don't think this dog could ever lead a normal life?"

Dr. Felder stared into space, much as Lolly J. was doing. "You never know, but I think the odds are against it." He looked inside Lolly J.'s mouth. He listened to her heart. He moved her tail aside to feel her belly. "I'll tell you one thing, though. You've got a healthy dog here."

"Good. But what about her right ear?" asked Olivia. "It smelled strange this morning and had some nasty smelling goop coming out."

Dr. Felder turned over Lolly J.'s ear flap. He took a moment to study the tattoo. "The ear looks fine. Who knows? Dogs get into things."

The three humans dropped into the silence that collected around Lolly J.

Finally, the vet broke the silence. "I've seen dogs protect themselves like this their whole lives." He put his hand on Lolly J.'s back. "This is the most extreme case I've seen, I'd have to say. She's really disconnected."

"I'm the one who's supposed to help her socialize," said Olivia. "I can't believe it, but I think she's made some progress. She howled this morning."

"That's what hounds do." Dr. Felder smiled.

"But she's been mute all her life. She saw a rabbit, and she howled like crazy." Olivia put her hand next to Dr. Felder's on Lolly J.'s warm fur.

"Well, that could be a beginning," the vet admitted. "But remember, her problem isn't communicating with animals. If she lived all summer at a shelter with people running around and she's still petrified, I don't know how much she's going to change. What does Lynn think?"

"She thinks she can be saved," Olivia informed him, "because she was a mother. All she needs is a pack leader to make things familiar and predictable."

Dr. Felder shook his head. He eased his hand off Lolly J.'s back. "What I love about Lynn is that she's an optimist." He looked Olivia straight in the eye. "It takes a lot to break an animal's spirit. And I think that's what's happened here." His voice cracked.

The three of them watched Lolly J. jerk her head back and forth to monitor the room. They watched her focus on the light streaming in the window. She seemed to melt into a beam herself, to abandon all threats, all mysteries.

Dr. Felder continued. "Imagine if no one paid attention to you until you were all grown up. Would you suddenly be normal?"

"No. I'd probably be really depressed. I'd be ignorant and really angry," said Olivia.

"Well, dogs don't often get angry. They get lost." Dr. Felder patted Olivia's hand. "But, if you're really determined, if you can find the patience, then maybe you can save this dog. Maybe you can make her feel secure enough to come to earth and be your friend. Who knows? It would be really cool. And it would be very admirable. It would be one of the hardest things you'll ever do in your life, but one of the most rewarding."

"I know what you mean," said Olivia. "She stepped on an acorn out front, and she totally freaked. Like it was a bomb."

"Well, now she knows she can survive stepping on an acorn," Dr. Felder joked. "It's all about her survival instinct. That's all she's had to keep her going. Tomorrow, when an acorn falls, maybe she'll think, 'Hey, that's two acorns now, and they didn't kill me. Maybe I can survive a third.'" Then, one day, she won't go bonkers at the sight of an acorn. Most people don't have the time or patience for a dog like this."

"We want to try," Mrs. Palmer declared.

Dr. Felder took Lolly J. off the table and placed her on the floor. She started sniffing the dogs and cats who had been there before her.

"Who knows? She may just surprise us." Dr. Felder pointed to a white party hat on his desk. "Norman's family gave that to me this morning. Norman's a cat. He turned nineteen today. They found him in a tree when he was a kitten. He was clueless and trying to survive. His family was patient, and Norman bloomed." Dr. Felder handed the leash to Olivia and gave Lolly J. a final pat. "I wish the best for all of you. Just remember, it'll be up and down."

Olivia and Mrs. Palmer thanked the vet. Olivia picked up Lolly J. and carried her outside.

"I liked that table," Lolly J. told Dottie as they zigzagged to the car. "It was cool and smooth like the laboratory's. And I liked that man. He smelled like a dog. He understands me."

"How do you know he understands you?" asked Dottie, hiking up from Lolly J.'s ear canal.

"By the way he touched me. It's like he's a dog. He wasn't petting me. He was joining me. It's hard to explain."

"Maybe he's a dog wizard."

"What's a dog wizard?"

"Someone who understands the inside of dogs," explained Dottie as Olivia put Lolly J. into the crate. "And I think he tells humans what you're thinking."

"I hope so."

CHAPTER 21. SQUARE CORNERS

When Olivia and her mother got home, Mr. Rosas was installing a fence in the backyard. A younger man stood nearby.

"I'm making the holes deep," said Mr. Rosas. "The bottom of the fence will be way underground," he assured Mrs. Palmer as he shoveled dirt. "It'll be like a fort. She'll never dig herself out."

"That's great, Dad!" said Mrs. Palmer. "Lolly J. can explore and get used to things!"

Olivia held Lolly J.'s leash while the dog sniffed the legs of the new man.

"Livie, I want you and your mom to meet my friend, Rhett. He trains dogs. I'm just an amateur. So now you have the best. I told him we have an emergency on our hands."

"Oh, wonderful! This is terrific," said Mrs. Palmer. "You've got quite a challenge here."

Rhett nodded shyly. He shook Mrs. Palmer's hand and then Olivia's. He reached down and patted Lolly J. on the head. "Hey, pup," he said, easily getting the dog's attention. "Let's see you guys do your thing. Take a little walk."

The trainer was friendly but serious. He looked through his glasses with intense interest as Lolly J. and Olivia began their zigzag around the yard.

"You do have quite a challenge here!"

"Yes, I do," said Olivia, lurching.

"I talked to Lynn. Your dog is intriguing, that's for sure." Rhett bent down and offered the back of his hand to Lolly J. when she and Olivia approached.

The dog sniffed and then looked away.

"You know what? She is observing more than you could possibly imagine."

"Like what? She seems so out of it."

"Did you see her tremble when she went toward the driveway?"

"Yes. Like she saw a ghost. She won't walk on part of the driveway."

"Look across the street at the point exactly opposite the place where she gets nervous."

Olivia and her mother looked across the street. An unhappy boxer was sitting at the edge of her own driveway.

"That's Lady," said Olivia. "They just got an invisible fence thing. It zaps her so she won't go in the street. She doesn't like it."

"Lolly J. knows Lady doesn't like it," observed Rhett. "She knows something scary is going on over there. So, to protect herself, your smart dog has extended the danger zone into her own world exactly opposite, right down the middle of the driveway! There's a safe side and a scary side." Rhett gave a thumbs-up sign. "Awesome!"

"Wow!" Olivia perked up. "She's like Sherlock Holmes!"

"She's so sensitive!" declared Mr. Rosas.

"So smart!" exclaimed Mrs. Palmer. "Let's just hope she doesn't see danger everywhere." She wished them good luck and then went into the house.

"Yes, your dog is very sensitive," Rhett told Olivia, "and very observant."

"Maybe that will help me socialize her," Olivia suggested.

Rhett grinned. "It may help. But she's not ready for friendship yet. First, she needs a routine so things start to make sense."

"I guess friendship is the last thing on her mind," said Olivia.

"Yup," said the trainer. He took Lolly J. to the acceptable part of the driveway and sat down next to her. "There's a great exercise for you," he said to the dog. "If you do it every day, you'll learn the most basic thing you need."

Lolly J. looked at him expectantly.

"Want to try?" he asked Olivia.

"Why not?"

Rhett replaced Lolly J.'s leash with a thin one about twice as long and handed it back to Olivia.

"And what is the basic thing this dog needs?" asked Mr. Rosas, listening closely beside the car in the driveway.

"It's learning that life with a human being doesn't have to be chaos. It can be predictable," said Rhett.

"That's what Lynn thought," said Olivia. "The predictability part must be pretty complicated."

"Not really," Rhett responded. "Think of it this way:

people have come and gone in this dog's life. But you're going to stay, Olivia. She'll see that you have some control over her. But we'll show her that she has some control, too."

Olivia looked away. "To be honest, I'm not sure I'm going to stay with this." She watched Lolly J. shake as she studied Lady across the street. "I do feel sorry for her. But we don't have an automatic connection. I thought that's why dogs become our pets, because there is a connection."

"The connection you see between most dogs and their owners only *seems* automatic, Livie." Rhett reached over and untangled a knot on the long leash. "It's because most dogs start being friends with people as soon as they're born." He ran a finger affectionately down Lolly J.'s snout.

"Even simple, everyday things, she has no clue about," Rhett explained. "Like if you put on your coat. She doesn't know that means you're going out. When you go out, she doesn't know whether you'll be gone forever. She doesn't know when to worry or when she can relax."

The dog wandered toward the garage and fixated on a clump of leaves. Keeping a good grip on the leash, Olivia followed while Lolly J. sniffed the leaves intensely.

"She'll be comfortable with leaves and cars and things soon enough," predicted Rhett. "But unless we help her, she won't know she can understand us. Right now she either worries or floats. 'Dubbity-dubbity do,'" he mimicked, gawking at the sky with his eyes wide.

"Worrying can fry your brain," said Olivia. "That's why I want a happy dog. I've had enough worry."

"But wouldn't it be sweet to make her happy?" Rhett asked.

"I want to be happy, too."

"I understand. I just so admire your giving this dog a try. When you don't grow up with something, it feels foreign. Like if a baby grows up with a wolf family, it thinks humans are strange."

Olivia laughed. "What baby would grow up with a wolf?"

"It has really happened!"

"Wow! That is so weird!"

"Livie, don't think about the wolves now," pleaded her grandfather. "You can research it later. Let's learn the exercise. I'll help you."

"Good," said Rhett. "Okay, your job is to lead your dog around."

Lolly J. had strolled onto the driveway and extended the leash as far as it would go.

"This is crazy long!" Olivia giggled.

"It *is* crazy long," agreed Rhett. "But with her normal leash, if she lags behind, the chain will tighten too quickly. She'll think, 'Oh, there's nothing I can do about this! I'm going to get strangled just for taking a walk.' With the longer one, she has time to decide whether to follow you or let the chain tighten."

"Interesting. Should we go to the sidewalk?" asked Olivia.

Rhett smiled. "No. Too many street noises. She'll freak."

"I know what you mean." Olivia walked onto the grass. The dog hovered over an invisible discovery in a crack in the driveway.

"All right, I want you to imagine a big square. It goes from the garage along the shrubs to the tree, forward to the back porch, sideways to the driveway, and then back to the garage," said Rhett. "I want you to walk along the sides of this square, and when you get to a corner, count to ten. Then, no matter where she is, no matter what she's doing, make a sharp turn down the next side. And keep going. That's it. Whether she is near or far, keep walking the square and stop at the corners. It's her responsibility to come along."

"But she doesn't know that. What if I accidentally jerk her when I turn?"

Mr. Rosas walked over to his granddaughter. "You will not hurt her, sweetheart. Her neck is strong. You will wake her up! Do you know how hard it is to train a dog, Livie? Particularly a deprived dog who does nothing but daydream or try to eat a whole turkey?"

"I guess it's almost impossible to train a dog like this, Grandpa."

"You're right," said Mr. Rosas. He gave Olivia a hug. "Dogs weren't born to walk on a leash any more than humans were. But we have to start somewhere. They like routines, and they like bosses."

Olivia tugged softly on the leash. Lolly J., continuing to examine the crack, did not respond.

"Oh, Grandpa, we should let dogs be wild the way they used to be. This is ridiculous."

"It's too late for dogs to be wild, Livie," said her grandfather. "Just walk. Dogs depend on humans now. If you put Lolly J. in a forest, she wouldn't like that either."

"You got that right," Rhett agreed, eyeing his stubborn client, who was still investigating an unseen wonder in the driveway.

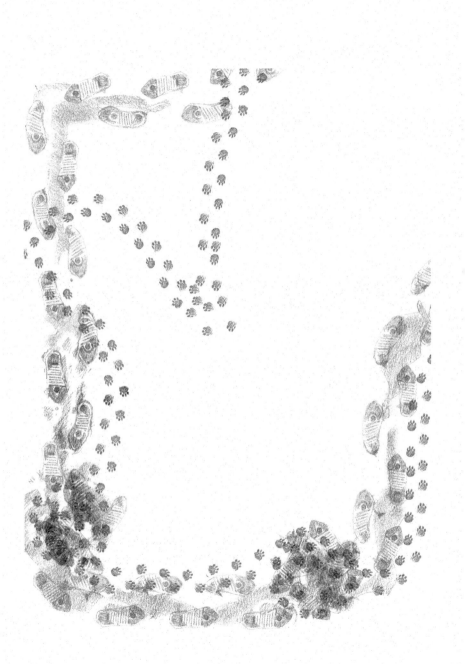

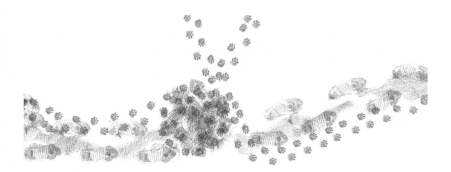

CHAPTER 22. TRAINING

"Walk toward the tree," Rhett called to Olivia.

She walked slowly across the yard. The leash was so long that it had not yet begun to tighten Lolly J.'s neck chain. The dog was now studying a ketchup-smeared napkin that had blown her way.

Olivia turned to get the dog's attention.

"Don't look at her. Keep going," Rhett coached.

Olivia continued toward the tree. The leash extended nearly its full length, about as long as two cars. Lolly J. had to jump forward, as though she'd received an electric shock. She looked hard at Olivia, who ignored her. The dog took a couple of steps toward the tree, but that was all.

When Olivia reached the tree, she stopped.

"It's been ten seconds. Start walking!" Rhett called.

"I'll choke her! She is so stubborn!"

"Start walking!" Mr. Rosas echoed.

"Okay. Okay." Olivia walked toward the house. Lolly J., feeling the pull again, broke into a quick zigzag.

When Olivia reached the house, she stopped. The dog stopped, too, but she was still nearly the length of the leash away as she tried to approach the tree. She gazed at Olivia again.

"Turn sharply and walk!" called Rhett.

"I hate this!" Olivia turned toward the driveway. Lolly J. lost her balance and landed on her behind.

"What is going on?" Dottie cried. "It's like a roller coaster in here. I need some food, or I'll be seasick! Please let me off."

"You'll have to wait," said Lolly J. "The girl has gone crazy. All this pulling is irritating my neck. She makes me fall down. I can't get where I'm going. There's a message from the Labrador, but I can't get near it. She is dragging me. If I go to a shrub to let you off, it'll squeeze my neck."

"Oh, Lolly J. She's trying to train you!" Dottie informed the dog.

"To do what?"

"To walk."

"Can't they see that I can walk?" asked Lolly J. in disbelief, picking herself up.

"This is good!" Dottie said. "The girl wants you to walk like her so you can walk with her."

"Why don't *they* learn to walk like *me*?"

"Whoa! Who's talking like a diva now? I tell you, trust me. Some things they teach you. Some things you teach them. In the end, it all works out."

"Okay. Okay. Ouch!"

"Are you hurt?"

"Not really. The girl pulled me again! Oh! She is interrupting my walk! I can't get to the tree!"

"You must go to her. She is your master," Dottie said firmly. "She's organizing you. You need organizing! You'll love it. If you go to her, she'll still take you to the tree to pee. She'll always take you to the tree, just maybe not right now. Go to her!"

"I'm going. I'm going. I don't like that pulling." Lolly J. trotted to Olivia's side as she left the house for the driveway.

"Olivia! This is an amazing moment!" shouted Rhett. "Keep going. Walk to the garage."

Olivia wrapped the slack of the leash around and around her wrist. She walked up the driveway toward the garage. Lolly J. stayed at her side.

When they reached the door, Rhett and Mr. Rosas were there to greet them. Mr. Rosas had tears in his eyes. "Brava, bella!"

"Oh, Grandpa. This was so hard for her!" Olivia knelt and stroked Lolly J.'s head. "Good girl!"

"Hear them?" said Dottie. "They're going nuts over you. I tell you, you give up something, she'll give you something. Here it comes. I can smell it."

Olivia gave Lolly J. a treat.

"It tastes good," said Lolly J. "But you know what else I like? She knew what she

142

wanted, and she let me know. No one ever let me know anything, except for the shelter woman."

"The shelter woman's different, though," said Dottie just before takeoff. "She's not yours."

"Right. But the girl is mine." Lolly J. flicked her head in a circle of delight.

"Why did she come to me?" Olivia asked Rhett.

"You were decisive, and you were confident. And, truthfully, your tugs on her neck annoyed her." Rhett whisked off his baseball cap and smoothed his hair. "Way to go! Now she has a chance to be decisive and confident, too. This dog has a chance!"

"We will do this every day after school," said Olivia. "I'm psyched."

"I'll work with her every morning," Mr. Rosas promised. Then he smiled. "Just a little bit, so she knows I'm not the boss."

"What a pack!" Rhett beamed.

"She really wants me to be next to her," Lolly J. reported, taking Dottie to the shrubs for a quick nibble.

"Yes. Humans and dogs need to walk side by side," Dottie confirmed. She slurped some aphids.

"Then when do I sniff?"

"You'll work it in," Dottie assured her as she landed back on the foxhound's ear. "Humans look at their word-mail, and you smell your pee-mail. Everyone knows that."

CHAPTER 23. MYSTERIES OF LIFE

After lunch, Olivia, her mother, and Lolly J. drove to the pet store. An abundance of animal scents and treat smells greeted them. The front door was glass, hiding nothing, so Lolly J. entered easily.

Mrs. Palmer went to a machine to print out a dog tag. Olivia looked at collars and selected a black one with white polka dots. Then Lolly J., fixating on one scent in particular, followed it with her nose to the ground. She pulled Olivia up and down the aisles until they were both running.

The foxhound rounded a corner and came face-to-face with the source of the scent. It was inside an open black box on wheels. Lolly J. hoisted herself up, placed her front paws on the edge of the box, and peered in.

Underneath the hood was an unforgettable sight. Someone she knew was lying in there, his body covered with a blanket and his head resting on a pillow.

"I say, is that you, foxhound?"

"I know that voice!" cried Dottie.

"It's Henry!" announced Lolly J. "He's wearing a hat!"

"Oh, I have to see this!" Dottie moved to get a good view. "Oh, no! Henry's in a baby's bonnet! In a baby carriage! Mr. Bottsford! You look absolutely smashing! Have you been shopping in London? If I keep laughing this hard, I am going to spew aphid juice!"

"I had no say!" shouted Henry. "My life is in ruins!"

"Get down! Get down!" The order came from a pair of red lips beneath a puff of white cotton-candy hair. "This is my new dog, and he needs his space!"

Lolly J. recognized the wet-broom scent. This woman had tried to take Lolly J. from the shelter, too!

"Come on, Lolly J.," scolded Olivia. "You need to get down." She lifted the dog's paws off the carriage and whispered to Lolly J., "This lady is crazy. She thinks that dog is her baby!"

Then Olivia looked at Henry and addressed the woman. "How cute. Your dog, is he too old to walk?"

"He can walk. But he's had a hard life," the woman replied. "I'm going to pamper him in his old age, just the way someone should pamper me." She took a flowered handkerchief from her purse with her red-stained hands and wiped Henry's mouth.

The bulldog squirmed. "Foxhound, you must come very soon. Follow my scent! You must save me, or I will die of embarrassment. I want to die a natural death! Please, save me!"

"I'll find you," Lolly J. called back as Olivia led her down the aisle. "Promise."

In the car on the way home, Lolly J. was fidgety in her

new collar. Olivia and her mother heard her tags clinking.

"This dog sure is an expert at shaking," moaned Olivia. "This morning I thought we had some hope. Now she's backsliding already."

"She's needy and inexperienced. She's not going to stop shaking in one day," responded her mother.

"Whatever." Olivia fiddled with her hair. "I guess she needs us but doesn't really want us. I can feel her isolation without even looking at her. Do you think we should keep her?"

"What do you think?" her mother asked back.

Olivia turned and looked at Lolly J., who was making loud licking sounds as she flicked her tongue on her leg. "You know she's not my dream dog, Mom. I thought maybe she was going in a different direction when she howled this morning. But I guess she likes to do that stare thing or to freak out, mostly. None of that is pet behavior, you know? How can I teach her the million things she needs to know? How can we know what's going to happen to her?"

"We can't know," said her mother, guiding the car out of a traffic jam.

"That's life, right?" mused Olivia, looking out the window. "We can't know anything for sure. Like whether the sun will even come out."

"Yes. The mysteries of life," said her mother, turning on the headlights beneath a darkening sky.

Olivia continued. "But the thing is, I don't think she's ever going to like me. The only thing she knows about me is that I jerked her around the yard. And how can I be a pack leader and teach her anything if she doesn't even know what a pack is?

Plus, Dr. Felder thinks she's too far gone anyway."

"He wasn't absolutely sure. And I'm not so sure," Mrs. Palmer reminded her.

Olivia looked at her mother's tired face. Mrs. Palmer was trying to liven up that face for the sake of a dog.

"Maybe she yearns for a pack even though she doesn't know exactly what one is or how to find it," said her mother.

"This is starting to feel like a job," Olivia groaned. "I'm just a kid who wants to play with a dog. Maybe get a kiss once in a while."

"Livie, it's up to you. We can get you a cute, happy, playful dog. Would you like that?"

"I don't know! I guess part of me thinks it would be amazing to get this weird dog to feel good."

"Maybe training Lolly J. *will* be like a job, with lots of hard work," her mother admitted. "But, as Dr. Felder said, maybe you'd feel like you were doing something that matters."

Olivia turned around again. Lolly J. was looking out the window with a worried expression. "How can I teach you not to be afraid?" she whispered.

The dog kept looking out the window. She was coming to like the sound of the girl's voice. But she had no way to tell her.

"What do you do if a dog doesn't learn?" Olivia wanted to know.

"Keep teaching anyway," replied her mother. "Deep down, they want consistency. Keep on teaching, keep on walking. And no matter what, keep on hoping."

While the girl and the woman talked, Lolly J. savored Henry's scent. It was on her paws. She had loved tracking him in the store. Until then, she hadn't had time to miss him.

As strange as that old bulldog was, he and Dottie were Lolly J's family. There was a hole without him. He had been hard on her, but he had believed in her. She had to save him.

CHAPTER 24. TAMING

When they arrived home, Olivia took Lolly J. to the tree, and Lolly J. took Dottie to the shrubs. However, before Dottie had a chance to finish her dinner, Olivia pulled the dog through the back door. She held the leash by the bowls, but the dog was too upset to eat or drink much, so they headed upstairs. Lolly J. made a beeline to her crate.

"Oh, dear. You look out of it again," Olivia observed. "This sure is up and down. Okay, go back to your mysteries. I'm going to supper with Mom and Grandpa. I don't think Grandma will come back until you're normal."

Lolly J. wanted the girl's voice and breath to stay near her. But the dog looked away. There was no way to tell the girl about her worries, about her lost friends. How was she going to find Henry? And now Dottie was stranded in the shrubs. She hoped the girl would stay with her, but Olivia walked out and closed the door.

In a while, though, she returned. She stood in the doorway with her mouth open in shock. The room had been transformed. The rug in the middle was strewn with pieces of whitish-gray confetti.

Lolly J. sat quietly in the crate and looked out at the scene.

"What have you done?" moaned Olivia. She had forgotten to latch the crate door. The dog looked away. A hot-dog chew toy lay untouched by her side. Olivia scooped up a handful of the confetti. There were words on the little bits of paper.

Lolly J. had chewed up a book! Olivia looked around frantically to see which one was gone. The spine of the book was resting in the rubble. She picked it up. It was *The Little Prince* with a half-chewed-up cover hanging off of it.

"No! No! This is not possible!" she wailed. "Lolly J., this is my most favorite, most precious book! How could you? I hate you!" Olivia began to sob. Clutching what was left of *The Little Prince* to her heart, she threw herself on the bed.

Olivia looked at the remains of her book. The first page had miraculously stuck to the cover. The page was nearly whole. She gently removed it. There were the words her father had written: "Happy Birthday! For my dear Olivia, who I am happy lives not on her own star but right here with us." She sat up, still crying, and looked at Lolly J. The dog was licking her thigh as though nothing had happened. "I wish I *did* live up in the sky like the little prince on his very own planet, far, far away from you!"

Lolly J. didn't look up.

"How could I have given you Daddy's *J*? What a joke!"

The dog looked up this time. She could tell the girl was sad. She felt sad for the girl. She loved the girl's scent so much that she'd wanted to taste it, devour it, from that stack of papers.

Olivia hurled the tattered spine to the floor. She stomped out into the hall and screamed down the stairs. "Lolly J. ate *The Little Prince*! She ruined Daddy's book!"

In a minute, her mother rushed up the stairs. Olivia was sobbing again. Mrs. Palmer took her daughter into her arms. "I'm sorry. I was in the basement. What happened?"

They sat on the bed together, and Mrs. Palmer looked down at all the bits of pages and what was left of the cover.

Olivia cried into her mother's sweater. "I can't take this!"

"Oh, dear. She's done an awful thing," said her mother, pushing back strands of Olivia's hair. "But maybe you're being too hard on her. She doesn't know what she did is awful. Remember what Rhett said. She doesn't know the meaning of what she does."

"Oh, Mom! Well . . . *I* know what it means!" Olivia hardly had the breath to get her words out.

"This is what we talked about in the car. This is the hardest part of your job, Livie." Mrs. Palmer massaged the tight muscles in the middle of her daughter's back. The sobs faded to sniffles.

"It's like a thousand fortune cookies," said Olivia, surveying the remains of *The Little Prince*. She leaned down and picked up a scrap. "'You are beautiful, but you are empty,'" she read. "I know what that is. That's what the little prince says to the roses when he falls to earth. He says they are empty because they haven't been tamed, and because they have never tamed anyone."

"Hmm," said her mother.

Olivia wiped her eyes. "The roses don't know what it means to be alive," she explained. "But the little prince's own

153

little flower on his own planet knows what it means to be alive because the little prince tames it. And when it's tamed, it grows to love him."

"That's a pretty wild message, Livie, considering what's happening right now."

"Yes, it is weird that I picked that one." Olivia looked at Lolly J. She was licking a paw.

"Is taming when an animal starts to love you?"

Mrs. Palmer pondered. She, too, watched Lolly J.'s pink tongue flip in and out of her mouth as she moved from one toe to the next. "Yes, you could say that taming is when they go from the world of animals to the world of people and are comfortable. They aren't afraid or aggressive. And love usually comes out of it."

"This dog will never be tamed. She's stuck," declared Olivia.

Mrs. Palmer wiped her daughter's thin, pale face with her hand. "Why do you love this book so much?"

"Because no one in it likes being alone."

"Well, I am going to find my copy." Mrs. Palmer got up and left the room. Olivia and Lolly J. sat in silence.

When Mrs. Palmer returned, she was holding *The Little Prince,* by Antoine de Saint-Exupéry, open before her. "I had this when I was your age, you know. And I loved it, too. I'm going to give it to you." She sat next to her daughter again. "Here's the part where the fox talks to the little prince about taming. Do you want to hear it?"

"Lolly J. needs to hear it."

"Okay. I'll read it to Lolly J." Mrs. Palmer looked directly at the dog, now sitting with her head bowed, and read,

*To me, you are still nothing more than a little boy
who is just like a hundred thousand other little boys.
And I have no need of you. And you, on your part,
have no need of me. To you, I am nothing more than
a fox like a hundred thousand other foxes. But if you
tame me, then we shall need each other. To me, you will
be unique in all the world. To you, I shall be unique in
all the world. . . .*

Mrs. Palmer looked up. "Olivia, the fox begs the little prince to tame him. I bet Lolly J. is dying to be tamed. Deep down I bet she wants to love you."

"You heard Dr. Felder. She's hopeless," Olivia declared once again. "She doesn't understand these words."

"That's the easy way out, Livie—to believe she's hopeless." Mrs. Palmer's voice was strong. She got up and went to the crate. For a moment, she watched Lolly J., who lay there with her eyes closed. Then she turned back to Olivia. "Don't you forget what happened today. Don't you forget that this lost dog ended up at your side. And this is just the first day! Do you remember what the fox says is the one necessary thing for him to be tamed?"

"What?"

"Are you ready for this? Patience."

"Patience! Patience? This is going to take my whole life!" Olivia grumbled. She got off the bed and joined her mother next to the crate. She looked down at Lolly J., who appeared to be sleeping. "We have to practice walking down stairs. We have to teach her about Lady's stupid fence that she can't even see. We have to walk in an invisible square. All this for a dog who is supposed to be a detective. But she has no mind! She's scared out of her mind!"

"Yes, you're right," said Mrs. Palmer. "Her mind needs a chance to return. You know, she's not sleeping at all. Look how tense her neck muscles are. She's just hiding from this complicated world."

Olivia and Mrs. Palmer stood beside the dog for a time. She fidgeted in a half-sleep and dreamed that she saw Dottie wailing in the dark on a twig of holly. When she opened her eyes, they met Olivia's.

"If you're going to learn anything," said the girl, "I have to find the patience to give you days—no, months—no, *years* of understanding. I don't think you know how much training and taming you need."

Lolly J. listened to every word, although she looked away.

"I was not born patient, Lolly J. If I am going to tame you, I will have to teach myself patience."

Something is wrong, thought the dog. She knew by the tone of the girl's voice.

"You have such a sweet face, but you are a difficult dog," Olivia told her.

Lolly J. looked at her again. She wanted the girl to keep talking. She blinked. "This is my master," she told herself.

Olivia turned back to her mother. "She needs me, doesn't she?"

"Yes." Mrs. Palmer leaned into the crate and gave the dog a pat.

Olivia knelt and gave the dog her attention. Lolly J. stood up. Something important was happening. She needed Dottie to help her understand the girl's wet blue eyes.

"We're going out," Olivia told Lolly J. "And then I'll clean this all up." She reached in and put the leash on the dog. Lolly J. slid forward.

Olivia picked up the book carcass and held it in front of Lolly J.'s face. "You ate my most precious treasure. It really, really hurts." She put her finger on the dog's little island spot and pressed it hard.

CHAPTER 25 . DOUBT

After *The Little Prince* incident, Olivia provided basic care to Lolly J. but nothing more. She took the dog outside to do her business, put fresh kibble and water in her bowls, and fastened her securely in the crate.

The next day, Sunday, Olivia did not practice the square with Lolly J. Instead, she ignored the inhabitant across the room and read at her desk. She was researching a seed bank in England, where scientists froze seeds from all over and saved them in underground vaults in case a catastrophe wiped out the world's plants.

After lunch with her mother, Olivia walked the three blocks to her grandparents' house. She often visited on weekends. Together, they weeded the vegetable garden, raked leaves, shoveled snow, or organized the basement or attic. It was a sunny, crisp fall day. As Olivia walked up the driveway to the backyard, her jaw dropped. Bright yellow leaves were falling like snow off the towering tree near the back porch. Her grandmother, tall and slender, was dancing in the middle of the downfall with her arms outstretched.

Olivia ran to her grandmother. "I can't believe it! The ginkgo is shedding, Grandma, and I'm here! I've never seen it!"

"Oh, hello, darling. I'm so happy you're here. Yes, yes! Isn't it beautiful?" Mrs. Rosas reached out her long arms and hugged Olivia tight as the leaves fell on them. "I was going to call you, but I thought the monster might need you." She kissed the top of Olivia's head.

Olivia wiggled out of the embrace to look her grandmother in the eye. "The monster can take care of herself this afternoon," she said. "I don't want to talk about her." She scooped up a handful of the odd triangular leaves and looked up at the tree. "It will be bald by tonight, right?"

"Yes, my *bonita*. All the leaves come off in one day. It is the most amazing thing."

"Does Grandpa know?"

"Yes. But he had to go help someone plan a porch. He promised. I don't think architects retire, really."

"Too bad," said Olivia.

"Yes. But he's seen it before. And you haven't. I am so happy you are here with me."

"Me, too. I'll help you rake them. You know, I read about why the leaves fall at the same time. It's unique," said Olivia as she stretched her own arms out in the leaf shower. She picked a leaf off her sleeve and fingered the stem.

"Livie, don't think about all that just now. Give your brain a rest. Come dance with me. Try to get out of yourself for a moment, my sweet." Her grandmother reached out to take Olivia's hands.

Olivia pulled her arms to her sides. "Get out of myself?"

"Yes, darling. I think you are tense. You are preoccupied with your pup."

"Well, I don't need to get out of myself! I am not even in myself!" Olivia responded in a loud voice. She stepped away from her grandmother.

"Oh, dear." Mrs. Rosas shook her head. She wiped the leaves off her shoulders. Her long face, which still had the beauty of the ballerina she once had been, frowned. "Your doggy has made you *loca*."

"I am not crazy!" shouted Olivia.

"Bonita, bonita! I don't mean to hurt you. I want to help you. It is like this: your dog is loca, and she is making you loca. That is what I see. I can see it in your eyes. And your mother told me about the book. I feel for you in my heart." She reached again toward her granddaughter to brush the leaves off her head, but Olivia moved farther away.

"Please leave me alone," requested Olivia. She dropped to the ground to avoid her grandmother's approach.

"Livie, what is happening to you?"

Olivia stretched out on the earth and closed her eyes. The yellow leaves fell on her softly. She moved her arms as if she were making angel wings in the snow. "I need quiet," she said.

"I see," said her grandmother. "You want to sulk? Well, if that is what you want, then sulk. I am going to rake these leaves."

Olivia did not answer. She remained on the ground with her eyes closed.

Her grandmother began to rake around her. "You are not talking? All right. Same here." Mrs. Rosas started to sulk.

In a while, dusk arrived, and the cold, hard ground was no longer a refuge. Olivia got up. She was covered with leaves. "These things get pretty stinky after a while," she said to her grandmother, who had amassed a few large piles.

"Oh, good morning, sunshine! Yes, they do get stinky if you leave them around. Did you research that, sweetheart? I mean it. I have always wondered about that. Why nature did that."

"I don't remember, Grandma," said Olivia. She looked up at the tree. Few leaves remained. She was a yellow snowman on a yellow carpet. She stomped around the tree to shake off the leaves. Then she picked up a rake that was leaning on the porch and joined her grandmother.

"I'm sorry I got weird," she said, starting to rake.

"I'm sorry I did, too," said Mrs. Rosas. "But sometimes a good sulk can clean you out. You start over." She wrestled with a bunch of sticky leaves on the prongs of the rake. "I was wondering. What about your tutoring? Are you still tutoring at school? I hear those little kids love you."

"No. I stopped," said Olivia.

"Oh, my. This is not a criticism. But I think that is the word for your life right now."

"What word?"

"*Stopped.*"

"Oh."

"Is it because you miss your daddy?" Mrs. Rosas cleared leaves around the picnic table.

With her rake, Olivia pulled down the leaves that clung to the tree trunk. "It started out with missing Dad," she said. "But now I realize everything is going to die. So what's the point, you know? I mean, that poor dog is going to die. She will probably be hit by a car. So I'm supposed to spend my life making her feel safe? The whole world is dying, really. There's a whole country that is practically drowning in the middle of the Pacific Ocean. Most people don't even know about it. It's tiny. It's drowning, Grandma!" Olivia placed her rake on the picnic table and sat on the bench.

Mrs. Rosas put down her rake, too, and sat next to her granddaughter. "Nature is confusing," she said. "It can be destructive, yes. You are a smart girl. No one can hide that from you. But not everything has to be a catastrophe. Maybe you can study and figure out how to save that little country that is drowning, Livie. Truly."

"Maybe someday," said Olivia, staring at the tree, just about bare now.

"I want you to remember this day. I want you to remember this tree," said her grandmother. "Put it in your heart. This tree is strong. Like you. Some ginkgos that were alive in ancient Greece are still alive, Livie! Socrates, or maybe Alexander the Great, climbed those same trees!"

"That's amazing, Grandma." Olivia put her head on her grandmother's shoulder. "But now everything is different from ancient times. Nothing lasts—except, maybe, plastic."

"Oh, yes?" remarked her grandmother quickly. "You know when the atom bomb dropped on Hiroshima and everything turned to dust? Grandpa told me about their gingkos. Those trees said, 'Oh, what was that? The biggest explosion in the history of the world? No problem! I will keep going.' Most of the other trees gave up, but not the ginkgos. That is you, Livie! You are strong. You used to run around full of energy, wanting to discover everything. Remember?"

"Yes, I do." Olivia got up. "It's getting dark. It's time for Lolly J. to go out. I better call Mom and ask her to do it. She expected me back by now."

"No, Livie. You go. You take her out. Your dog is waiting for you."

"What? You want me to go home to the monster? I thought you didn't like dogs."

Mrs. Rosas rose from the picnic table and walked with Olivia onto the back porch, where she turned on the light. "Sit," she said. "Just for a moment." They sat in the wicker chairs.

"I love dogs, Livie!"

"You do?!"

"Yes, I do." Mrs. Rosas took her granddaughter's hand.

"I just don't want you to have a crazy one, or an unsafe one. I don't want to fall down and break my hip. I don't want Grandpa to fall again. We are lucky he didn't break a bone."

"Grandma, I don't want you to break your hip either," insisted Olivia. "I think you're right to stay away from this dog. She is a calamity. This whole thing is a calamity. Mom wants her, and I want to help Mom. She's so sad. For a minute, I even thought Lolly J. and I could be friends. She came to my side. But she's too unpredictable."

"You know, Livie, you make me think of my dog," said Mrs. Rosas.

"You had a dog?"

"Yes, I had a dog when I was about your age."

"What kind of dog?"

"An Akbash."

"A what?" Olivia couldn't help chuckling at the strange name.

"An Akbash! You can laugh. But let me tell you, they are the best guard animals. And gorgeous. All white. Very grand. Almost as big as a Great Dane. They look like polar bears."

"Wow! And that was your dog, Grandma?"

"That was our dog on the farm. His name was Augusto. He guarded the sheep. And he guarded me. He was my best friend. My father used to let me go to town with Gusto. That's what we called him—Gusto."

"Do you have any pictures of him?" asked Olivia.

Mrs. Rosas had tears in her eyes. "No. You see, that is what I want to tell you. When the revolution was coming, when we knew there was going to be a lot of violence, we had to leave our home. We had to leave the country very quickly.

And we had to leave Gusto."

"Oh, Grandma! What happened to him?"

"I'm not sure." Mrs. Rosas's face looked pained. "I knew when I said good-bye to him that I was saying good-bye forever. But, of course, he didn't know that. We left him with another farmer, but nobody knows what happened to him."

Olivia had tears in her eyes, too. "That is so sad."

They sat for a moment in silence. Then Mrs. Rosas smiled at Olivia. "Dogs see us for who we really are," she said. "They see what we need. And they try to give it to us."

"Really?"

"Yes, truly."

"Even Lolly J., do you think?" asked Olivia.

"Well, when I met that dog, all I could think was, 'No, not this dog. This dog is an exception. She is too crazy.' But now I am thinking that maybe I was too hasty in my judgment. I think of Gusto. I am beginning to think that what happens to Lolly J. depends on one thing."

"What?"

"*Tú*, bonita! It depends on *you*, darling," said Mrs. Rosas. She stood up. "I think you need to get home to that dog."

"And do what?"

"Do what Grandpa says. You have to teach her how to be a dog with a person. Try, Livie, try."

"Maybe," said Olivia. She gave her grandmother a kiss and raced down the steps toward home.

CHAPTER 26. TRYING

Olivia couldn't stop picturing her grandmother as a girl with the enormous, affectionate Gusto by her side. The very next chance she had—after school the following day—she practiced walking the square with Lolly J. She put the long leash on the dog and they rushed out back.

In Olivia's excitement, she started out walking too fast. Lolly J. sniffed pee messages and lagged behind. But when Olivia slowed down to wait for Lolly J. and the dog stepped up her pace, that didn't work either, because Lolly J. had forgotten the point of the exercise: to join her master. They were so out of sync that Olivia just dropped the leash, and, safely contained by the new fence, they roamed the yard separately. *Lolly J. is no Augusto*, Olivia thought. *Can she ever be?*

Rhett the trainer, as well as Olivia's grandfather, joined them out back at times. As promised, Mr. Rosas walked the square with Lolly J. in the morning, while Olivia was in school. The yard became a battleground for patience.

"What's going on?" Olivia asked Rhett incredulously after a couple weeks of ups and downs. "I mean, I thought she caught on the first day. She can't keep anything in her head!"

"Well, the first day isn't every day," the trainer said calmly. "But it's an important day. Hang in there."

Olivia's concentration suffered because she kept the image of Gusto, the perfect companion, in her mind as she watched her own dog stumble around. And Lolly J.'s concentration suffered because Dottie had been missing for weeks since she'd gotten stranded in the shrubs. Sometimes Lolly J. imagined the ladybug sitting right on her snout. *Go when the girl goes. Stop when she stops*, she could hear Dottie say. But that didn't get Lolly J. to her master's side. She missed Dottie so much that she got frazzled.

Nonetheless, the foxhound tried her best, and slowly she learned the most convenient way to ease the pulling on her neck: she simply scrambled to Olivia's side before she could feel a tug. She did it again and again. And then, without fanfare, that special day arrived when everything came together and, just as Dottie had predicted, Lolly J. and Olivia *stayed* at each other's side.

There wasn't one moment when the girl and the dog finally fit together. Exactly how and when it happened was hard to pin down—as with the appearance of a first tooth or a first freckle. The connection was gradual, but once it happened, it changed everything.

I will stay next to you to make you happy, Lolly J. said in her mind to the girl. True, her neck felt better that way, too, but mainly she loved hearing Olivia's happy voice and gleeful clapping. She loved the "Good girl!" sound her master chanted with joy. And as she would tell Dottie, Lolly J., too, felt happier than she could remember.

Lolly J. and Olivia began to move as though they had been together always. They couldn't wait to see each other. Olivia would come home from school and run to Lolly J.'s crate. Then they would descend the stairs and speed out back. Outside, they continued practicing the square and walked up and down the spooky half of the driveway. Inside, they practiced going through doors. They roamed from room to room, over every threshold.

Sometimes Olivia shouted, "Oops!" and tugged gently upward on the leash, as Rhett had taught her. He'd let her choose her own word to get the dog's attention. Lolly J. had no idea why Olivia jerked the chain and sounded like a wounded animal, but the dog *did* know Olivia was annoyed. She was just starting to feel some confidence, and *wham*, the girl would shout at her.

Then it hit her. The dreaded "Oops!" came right after the foxhound did something; it never came when she did nothing. It happened when she stepped near the street, jumped on a table, slurped a sandwich off the counter, or put a book in her mouth. Maybe if she never did those things, the pull and the "Oops!" would go away.

Lolly J. experimented. When she and Olivia practiced going through the living room door, the dog crept up to a long, low table with a book on it. Then she crouched as if preparing to leap on the table. She opened her mouth as if preparing to devour the book. Olivia opened her mouth and formed a circle with her lips. *Yes, that's it!* thought Lolly J. *She is going to shout, "Oops!" She is still training me! She must make that sound when she is unhappy with what I do!*

In the end, the "Oops!" never left the girl's lips, because the dog neither jumped on the table nor touched the book. But Lolly J. gained invaluable information: she had the power to keep the chain from pulling, not only by walking a certain way, but also by behaving a certain way. She could be *good* at this training thing.

The dog's confidence reached the point where she felt comfortable enough to train her master in a crucial area. Sometimes Lolly J. had to pee so badly that she couldn't sit

or lie down; she had to do the little dance Henry had talked about. At those times, Olivia and her mother watched her with smiles on their faces and said, "How cute!" But they never took her outside.

So, Lolly J. decided to put her nose on Olivia's knee and jerk her head sideways, swiping her nose across the knee. Time after time, the girl leaned down and patted the dog on the head. The message wasn't getting through. Then, one day, during dinner, Lolly J. was sure she was going to have an accident. She felt the pressure of her pee about to burst. She ran beneath the kitchen table. She wiped her nose twice across Olivia's knee and then, unable to help herself, peed an enormous puddle beside the girl's feet.

"No! No! Lolly J.! You know better!" cried Mrs. Palmer, leaping from her chair.

Olivia reached down and grabbed the dog's collar. "Oops!" she said, giving an upward yank.

Oops?! thought Lolly J. *Oops? No, this is not my problem! This is your problem. You need to learn to take me out when I feel a flood coming!* She stood in the pee and immediately whisked her nose back and forth on Olivia's knee. Then she followed the girl to the back hall, where the girl quickly plucked the leash off its hook on the wall. Again, the dog rubbed her nose across the girl's knee. She did it again and again. Then she stood calmly and waited for her master to understand the gesture.

"Oh, I get it! I get it!" Olivia exclaimed. "You had to pee! You were telling me you had to pee! Mom, she was trying to tell us with that nose thing! She's training me!" Olivia bent down and put the leash on the dog.

Mrs. Palmer rushed to join them. "Oh, Lolly J., sweetheart!" she said. "You're communicating! I don't think we can say 'Good girl!' or you'll think it's okay to pee inside. I'll just clean it up, and that will be that. Next time you'll know that we got your message."

"Yeah, it takes time for *us* to learn, too," said Olivia as she escorted Lolly J. out the door.

The next day, Lolly J. got a big surprise as she and Olivia were practicing the square. The foxhound had joined Olivia at a corner in perfect fashion. She assumed that they were about to move on to the next corner. But Rhett, standing in the middle of the square, hollered something to Olivia, and instead of proceeding, the girl turned around and walked the other way, reversing their routine completely.

Stunned, Lolly J. stood at the corner. She didn't know whether to follow her master or to go in the direction that her training had drilled into her. *What would Dottie do?* she asked herself. *I can't figure this out. I was doing so well. I have been trained to go from the tree to the house, but my master is walking away from the house. She is going toward the garage!*

Olivia and Rhett gave all their attention to the dog. "This is a huge moment, Livie," said Rhett, excited. "What she does now will tell us whether she feels connected to you. It's one thing to walk the square like a robot. It's another thing to follow you wherever you go."

"How can she decide what's right?" whispered Olivia thoughtfully.

"It's hard to say," Rhett whispered back.

They waited. And Lolly J. waited. They were like three outfielders waiting for action in a baseball game. Lolly J.

looked at the back porch. Then she looked at the girl, who had stopped halfway toward the garage and was holding the long leash, now almost fully extended.

Lolly J. heard Dottie's voice in her head, loud and clear. *You must follow your master.*

The dog let out a quick purr of jubilation and flicked her head in a circle. Following her master was exactly what she wanted to do. Then she decided it was exactly what she was supposed to do. She bolted toward Olivia.

"She's coming, Rhett. She's coming!" Olivia clapped her hands and started to sprint to her dog.

"Stay where you are!" shouted Rhett. "Let her go to you!"

Olivia stopped and let Lolly J. complete her run. In a second, the dog stood beside her, her paws in line with the girl's feet, and looked up at her master. Olivia bent down to put her arms around the dog. "Good, girl! Good, girl!" she cheered. For a fleeting second, Lolly J. let the girl hold her. Then she stepped out of the hug.

"She's definitely your dog now, Livie. But she's still timid," called Rhett.

"Okay, okay," said Olivia, looking disappointed and separating from her dog.

Even though a hug still meant too much closeness, Lolly J. loved nothing more than walking the earth as Olivia's shadow. At first the foxhound had no idea about the word heel. But soon she knew that it meant putting her paw next to the girl's foot and walking with her in a straight line. Zigzags were history.

Safe at Olivia's side, Lolly J. got used to the horn blasts, squeaky brakes, and flashing car mirrors coming from the street out front. She savored the glorious meadow at the shelter, where they ran all the way to the flowers. She finally met a butterfly and named her Shy.

But the dog remained restless. Everywhere she went, she sniffed for Dottie and Henry. They were both still missing.

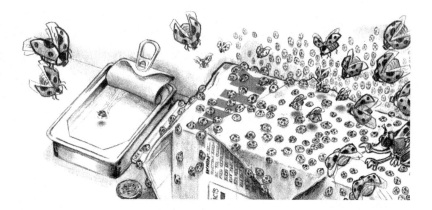

CHAPTER 27. STAGES

After dinner on a cold night, when Lolly J. and Olivia were out at pee time, the foxhound was sure she smelled Dottie's goo coming from the garage. She walked toward the door, which was open a crack. Yes, it had to be Dottie!

"You want to go in and explore? That's fine," said Olivia. "This is where Grandpa fixes things. It's cozy." She opened the door and turned on the light.

As soon as they entered, Lolly J. heard Dottie. "Lolly J.! Lolly J.! I'm over here! I'm behind the table!" she called from the far corner of the garage.

"Are you okay?" Lolly J. asked. "Oh, Dottie, please be okay!"

"I'm fine. Oh, I thought I'd never see you again! Once in a while I make goo for you. I couldn't make too much, or the man would spray us. I thought you'd never come!"

"Dottie, I've been looking for you everywhere. How did you get in here?"

"I came in on the man. It's a long story. Come on, drag

your leash over."

"But I'm with the girl. She needs me to be a good dog. I want to be a good dog for her. And she is patient with me. I walk well now. Wait until you see!"

"Wow, Lolly J.! You have come a long way!"

"A lot has happened. And I've missed you so much."

"I've missed you, too! Start sniffing. She knows you like to sniff. Come under the table to the corner."

Lolly J. sniffed beneath Mr. Rosas's table.

"You smell something good?" asked Olivia. "That's fine. Get used to it here. You're ready. I don't think you'll get scared."

Lolly J. walked to the other side of the table. She followed Dottie's voice to the corner, behind an old television that hid a thick black pipe running along the wall a few inches above the floor. The dog felt the heat of the pipe and noticed that a sea of ladybugs was scrambling all over it. It was a sea of Dotties! Well, not exactly. There was only one Dottie, and she was swimming under the pipe in a sardine tin.

"I'm in the pool!" Dottie called to the foxhound. "They insist I swim alone," she said. "I'm nearly one hundred—in ladybug years. I'm more than twice as old as these kids. They don't want to bump me." She looked up at her foxhound. "You kept me young, Lolly J.! So much activity! So much drama! Watch!" she said, showing off her backstroke. "You'd never know I had a hideous accident." She did a flip in the air. "Welcome to Hibernation Spa!"

"How did you find this place?" asked Lolly J. "It's beautiful!"

"What do you mean, *find* it? I established it!" Dottie

bragged. "When I couldn't find you, I had to do something to occupy myself. Come see." She swam to the edge of the tin and gestured toward the milk carton lying on its side beneath another section of pipe. "That's the beach." Lots of ladybugs sat perfectly still on a piece of sandpaper atop the carton. Each had a tiny, pale green eyeshade resting across its pin eyes.

"Sunglasses?" asked Lolly J. in amazement.

"No, silly. I give everyone a cucumber seed. It rejuvenates and refreshes the eyes, and it fits perfectly. They're all so excited to be here. They've never hibernated before. I was glad to do it for them. Make a party of it. A second hibernation is very rare for a ladybug. I thought I'd show them the ropes. Not that they need it."

"Because nature tells them what to do?"

"Right," commended Dottie. "Instinct tells them exactly what to do. You are such a good student. I told them all about you."

"I'd like to meet them sometime. Did they help you get your supplies?"

Dottie laughed. "Oh, no. There's a yellow Labrador down the street who helps me. His name is Ranger. He comes and keeps the man company sometimes. And he takes me out to eat."

"Oh, I like his scent! I want so much to meet him," said Lolly J. "Why don't I ever see him?"

"He comes in the middle of the day while you're in your room after you practice with the man," Dottie told her. "I ask him to bring any cucumber and raisin scraps that the man leaves. He is a retriever, after all. He found the sardine tin and the milk carton in the recycling container. We get the water from a drip. You have to be resourceful. I hope I've taught you that."

"Yes, you have, Dottie."

"Good! Let me see your face. You look more relaxed."

"I'm not as scared. The girl and I have a routine. I like that. There aren't so many mysteries anymore. I know the doors. I know the stairs. I know my bowls. I know the tree. I know the man who brings papers to the hole in the front door. I know creatures when we walk. I know the shiny things. I know the girl is there when I sleep at night."

"Wow! You sound almost normal!"

"Maybe. I don't know. I still get scared sometimes."

"Just take it as it comes," said Dottie.

Lolly J. watched Dottie float. That old ladybug made her so happy. "Dottie, it's not the same without you. I don't know how to love the girl. It's not like loving you."

"Well, be there when she needs you. That's what humans like. That's all."

"I'm not always sure when she needs me." Lolly J. faked a few sniffs to appear occupied while the girl arranged a stack of logs.

"She always needs you."

"Okay, okay. I'll try." Lolly J. watched Dottie slip and slide as she climbed up the side of the tin. "You look dried up. You're working too hard, Dottie. You need a break. Let me take care of you."

"I just need a good moisturizer. And my body isn't what it used to be," the ladybug lamented, leaning heavily on the rim of the tin. "I told you, this is my last hibernation."

"When does it start?"

"In a few weeks."

"You're going to sleep on the pipe?"

"Yes. It will be glorious."

Lolly J. couldn't imagine Dottie and her friends lying motionless in the garage for months and months.

"Will you be 150 years old after the hibernation?" asked Lolly J.

"I will be truly ancient, foxhound." Dottie's teeny eyes focused on Lolly J. "Please come over here for just a second."

Stretching the leash as far as it would go, Lolly J. inched toward Dottie.

"I might not wake up," Dottie stated solemnly from her delicate perch on the sardine tin.

"You mean you might die?" asked Lolly J., her eyes widening.

"Yes. I have always told you the truth."

Lolly J. looked at the floor. "But I can't live without you.

I love you too much for you to die."

"Come on, Lolly J. You need to pee," Olivia called.

"I have to obey the girl, Dottie. I *like* to obey the girl. But I can't leave you."

Dottie's eyes moistened. "Wow, so many feelings! But you've learned to put them into words. This is nothing like the trapeze. You're more magnificent than I ever dreamed."

"Thank you. I've had some experience. It helps. But it was easier before, I think. I didn't have feelings when I just shook." Lolly J. bowed her head. "How can I get hold of a good feeling and make it last? How can I ever be happy after you die?"

"Come to me, my foxhound."

Lolly J. lowered her head to the edge of the sardine tin. With all her might, Dottie propelled herself onto the dog's snout. Her shell, shining in the garage light, protected the bent wing underneath as she teetered. She looked into Lolly J.'s eyes. "You cannot always have what you want," the ancient ladybug said plainly. "Life doesn't work that way. If you want to eat everything in sight, then you end up with a stomachache. And a stomachache is not what you want."

"I see what you mean. So how *does* it work?" Lolly J. didn't mind at all that Dottie's legs were tickling her. She loved having the ladybug so close after her long absence.

"You have to take the sad with the happy." Dottie reflected a moment. "Remember how I told you a long time ago about the elephant I loved?"

"Yes. How could I forget?"

"Well, my elephant died. He was an amazing creature. Brilliant and loyal. He had great instincts. We worked at a circus, and oh, how I loved that circus! And I loved him. He made me daring. He encouraged me to be my outrageous self. But there was sadness, too. We couldn't eat meals together. Can you imagine?" She paused. "And then he died. But here I am! With my dancing legs on!"

"I'm sorry your elephant friend died," said Lolly J. "It's hard to take the sad with the happy, isn't it?"

"Of course it's hard! But it's something every creature has to learn to do. You don't get anywhere moping!" Dottie scrambled in a circle. "Get real!"

"I *am* real! I am a real dog!" Lolly J. shot back.

Dottie stood on her favorite place on Lolly J.'s snout. "Yes, you are. You are becoming real because you're learning what life is all about. You're learning who you are. I once knew a pigeon who thought she was a fly. I couldn't think of her as a real pigeon because she didn't think of herself as a real pigeon."

"Oh, Dottie, you just made that up."

"I did not! My whole life sounds made-up, but it isn't."

"Well, please come back to the Nine, just for a while. You can have a fur bed. And I'll take you to the shrubs. I need you, Dottie. And we'll find Henry. And you can tell me if you see a fox. I thought I found one, but it was a rabbit. I never told you."

"Oh, dear, that must have been disappointing. Of course I will go with you. I'll stay for a while," Dottie promised. "I'll commute to the spa. And yes, we must rescue Henry."

"We have to be quick," warned Lolly J. "The girl is pulling."

"Okay." Dottie addressed the spa. "I'm heading out with Lolly J. I'll be back. Have fun!"

Hundreds of ladybug messages rose in the air.

"Bon voyage!"

"Take care!"

"Don't worry about us!"

"We love you, Madame President!"

"Say hi to Lolly J.!"

Dottie disappeared under the dog's ear flap.

Lolly J. strode out of the garage beside Olivia and peed on a Ranger message. Then the three of them went inside.

That night, up in the bedroom, Lolly J. was content. Dottie was resting on the Nine, and Olivia was curled up in bed. The dog snuggled on her blanket in the crate. She glanced at the tiny pieces of the paper she'd chewed. They were now gathered in a see-through pink plastic bag next to the clock on the girl's table.

"I almost want to lie next to the girl," Lolly J. told Dottie. "But she might not want me."

"Stages," Dottie said. "Life comes in stages. You're looking at your next stage over there in that bed. You'll know when it's time to go to her. Trust me, I know stages. Before I became a dot, I was a jelly bean and then a little lizard-looking thing."

Lolly J. and Dottie laughed like they'd done in the old days. And then they fell asleep.

CHAPTER 28. A WHIFF OF HOPE

The next few weeks brought some big changes at 232 Clover Street. Lolly J. was giving up her dream that Dottie would live forever. Dottie was giving up her dream that Lolly J. would be completely independent by hibernation time. Olivia no longer dreamed that a dog could become your best friend without hard work and patience. And Mrs. Palmer no longer dreamed that a dog would ease the pain of her husband's death. Everyone was feeling better.

Lolly J.'s arrival affected the neighbors as well as the Palmer family. Mr. Macgill, who had dreamed of a quiet dog for his retirement, now wanted his own loyal shelter dog. A few kids on the block, who had little licky dogs, dreamed of a serious, mysterious one like Lolly J.

As for Lolly J., she was now comfortable going into the garage with Mr. Rosas after their walk each morning. Finally, she met Ranger. She first laid eyes on him when he was lounging at the spa and chatting with Dottie. He was a big, solid yellow dog. Lolly J. saw why she adored his scent. He was a mature dog, but he had the jolliness of a puppy. His face opened to her right away.

"I couldn't wait to meet you," she said, her heart beating fast.

"And I've wanted to meet you." Ranger stood to address his new friend. "I have been smelling your fear."

"Oh."

"But the scent of your messages tells me you're less afraid now. How are you doing?"

Lolly J. walked away from the spa to another corner of the garage so she could speak privately. Ranger followed. "I finally have a human," she whispered. "I have a name. I have a home. I have a best friend. And I have Henry."

"Sounds good to me," said the Labrador, lying down and listening attentively.

"But my best friend is going to die. My human needs love. And Henry is lost," Lolly J. explained. "I've been trying, but I'm still afraid sometimes. It's not like having too many doors. This is different. This fear comes from too many feelings. I can't tell what's going to happen."

Ranger wrinkled his face into a smile. He wagged his long, expressive tail and looked intensely at Lolly J. "I can't tell you what's going to happen. But I will take what's left of your fear, if you want. Give you a break," he offered with a wink.

"How do you do that?" Intrigued, Lolly J. lay down next to him.

"All you have to do is give it to me. I'm good at this. My lady takes me to sick people in hospitals to take their fear."

"Wow!"

The Lab steadied his eyes on Lolly J.'s "Don't think about it too much. That's what's so special about animals. We don't fill up with thoughts like humans do." He looked over at a frustrated Mr. Rosas trying to move around a large piece of wood under a ruler. "People need to chew on a good toy once in a while," he joked. "Pee outside. Chase a chipmunk."

He and Lolly J. had a good laugh.

"People think we love them," Ranger told her. "And we usually do. But the most important thing is that we calm them. And they love that."

"We have a lot of power, don't we?" reflected Lolly J.

"Yes, we do. It's sort of a secret. But not really. Sometimes I think humans worship us. It can be embarrassing. They build us hospitals and bakeries and hotels. What's next? Our own airplanes?"

Again they had a good laugh.

Ranger watched Lolly J.'s face light up. "You are such a solemn dog. But I think you're having fun."

"I am! I don't have fun often," Lolly J. admitted.

"Well, it's time to just be a dog! Make decisions without too much thought."

"I like to be quiet," Lolly J. confided. "I come from a laboratory where it was best to be quiet. Can I still be a real dog?"

"Of course. You are a dog, but you are also yourself."

"Good. I know most hounds howl all the time, but that's just not me. I am going to be like the skunk in the backyard who didn't like being stinky. He was okay with it."

Ranger nodded in approval amid the racket of Mr. Rosas's hammer and the whir of the ladybugs' gossip as they cleaned their elytra in the pool. "As long as you can howl when necessary," he advised. He flicked a piece of sawdust off his leg with his nose.

"Yes, I can," Lolly J. assured him. "I bet you can do a scary bark if you have to."

"Yes, I can—when necessary. But to tell you the truth, that part of being a dog doesn't interest me much."

"I know what you mean. I tried to be fierce once with Dottie, but it backfired. I don't have the hang of it."

"I like being fierce only as a very last resort," said the Lab, getting up and stretching his big back like a cat.

"It was an emergency," Lolly J. explained, "but I should have tried talking first."

"Well, now you know."

Lolly J. got up and strolled over to Mr. Rosas. She stood next to his table.

"What is it, sweetheart?" He stopped his work and looked down.

She opened her mouth, tilted her head back, and let out a giant howl: "A-OUUUUUU!"

The spa buzzed.

"Oh, my, bella!" exclaimed Mr. Rosas. "What's the matter? Do you hear something? Do you smell something? What are you trying to tell me?"

He put down his hammer, ran around the garage, and looked out the windows.

The ladybugs went silent.

"What is it, Lolly J.?" yelled Dottie.

"I had to practice. I have to be ready if I need to be fierce."

"Good grief!" Dottie scolded. "The whole spa is in an

uproar. They think it's the end of the world. We both know you're a great howler. Take it easy!"

"Well, it has been a while. I had to make sure," Lolly J. explained. "Please tell your friends I'm sorry."

"I will. Everything's fine, everyone! Lolly J. was just testing her equipment," Dottie announced to the spa.

Lolly J. saw that the man at the window was worried. She walked over, sat next to him, and put her ear to the side of his knee.

"I guess it's over, whatever it was." He patted her head and returned to the table.

"Talk about power. You upset everyone in one second," Ranger chuckled as Lolly J. trotted back to him.

"Well, it's good to know I can do that. It's easier to be calm—not as calm as you, of course. I have never met anyone as calm as you." She put her chin down on Ranger's paw and made herself comfortable. "Is it because you have no fear?"

"No. I have fear sometimes, when I need it. Your howl got my instinct going. I almost had to bark." Ranger chortled. Then he licked Lolly J.'s ears. She purred.

"Do you check the perimeter?" Lolly J. asked shyly.

"Of course I check the perimeter! I'm a dog! But I do it with hope, not fear. Hope makes things feel better. I don't know why. I don't think about it."

"I see." Lolly J. didn't quite understand either, but she didn't need to think about it. She was a dog. "So, if I give you my fear, will I have more calm and hope?" She jumped to her feet at the thought of it. "I've always had dreads and worries. Some were real; some I think I made up. You know, dreads and worries are good company sometimes."

"Oh, my dear Lolly J., you can keep your little dreads and worries. I'll just take what's left of that big fear that sits inside and eats away at you—the kind that keeps you up at night, the kind that makes you shake. You're done with that. It's like old skin ready to peel. When you sniff a rose bush, you'll still worry about the nuisance of getting a thorn in your nose. But you won't sweat the big stuff. When you sniff the girl, you won't lose sleep over what comes next. You've worked so hard; you should have some peace. This is the last step." Ranger's strong tail thumped on the floor.

"Yes!" Lolly J. sat up. "I will give you whatever is left of my big fear."

"Wonderful!"

Ranger placed his paws on hers. Lolly J. felt the warmth travel up inside her and tickle her back. She was as relaxed as a flower, as strong as a weed.

She bowed her head and thanked him.

"You're welcome." Ranger flashed his big grin. "Sometimes the most amazing things in life happen quickly if we're ready—and lucky."

"Wow. I want to be kind like you," said Lolly J.

"You are kind. To be kind when you have experienced so little kindness is unusual. You are an unusual dog."

"I seem to be."

They strolled together back to the spa.

CHAPTER 29. AN EMERGENCY

One snug afternoon in the garage followed another. Mr. Rosas worked at his table and sang. Dottie and her crew gossiped and hatched plans for a spa in every garage on the block. Lolly J. and Ranger talked philosophy, helped the ladybugs, and commanded a network of rabbits and squirrels who were on the lookout for Henry.

The rabbit from Mr. Macgill's yard was a great contact. His burrow was a few feet from the garage door. He spread the word to his hundreds of contacts, who were out collecting their dandelion and twig snacks for winter. Dottie named the rabbit Pronto.

The squirrels in Lolly J.'s tree were on alert, too. They combed the neighborhood for a bulldog in a hat while they looked for their nuts. Ranger, who went for long walks each morning with his lady, kept close watch around town.

If Henry was wandering about, there was no doubt one of the prowling detectives would send the news to the garage in a flash.

One day Ranger was antsy when he arrived. Lolly J. had never seen him like that.

"I've got some big news," he said, pacing.

"Really?" Dottie looked up from a raisin nibble on the beach. "From Pronto? He knows everything!"

"No. I did the legwork myself, with my lady."

"What do you mean?" asked Lolly J., pacing beside him.

"We passed a woman pushing a black thing. I smelled a dog. I ran my lady to it. A dog was lying in there! He had a hat on!"

"Was it Henry?"

"He called himself Bottsford. He said he's the only one of the woman's dogs who gets out because she's made him her baby. All the others are locked inside the house."

"Bottsford is Henry's last name! Was he a bulldog?" asked Dottie.

"I couldn't tell. He had a strange odor."

"Was he old, and did he have an accent?" asked Lolly J.

"Yes."

"That's Henry!" squealed Dottie.

"I thought so!" exclaimed Ranger.

"We have to go get him!" shouted Lolly J.

"Right away!" commanded Ranger. His muscular tail swished. His legs started to gallop in place. "All of the woman's other dogs are starving. All except for the one who's made himself king. Nestor. He used to be a nice Doberman, but now he stays inside all day and eats all their food, including the baby's—or Henry's. Old cat food. Henry says Nestor hates him. This is an emergency! We must go now!"

"Can the neighbors help?" Dottie teetered on the raisin with excitement.

"There are no neighbors. The house is in the middle of a field. I have a bad feeling about this."

"We have to get ourselves together here!" Dottie limped off her raisin and headed down the milk carton under the beach to get to the dogs.

"I am not a dramatic dog, Dottie," said Ranger. "You know that. But we have to go this minute. Who knows how long that Doberman will stay away from Henry? And those dogs can't go much longer without food!"

"Oh, dear! How do we get out of here?" cried Lolly J. Her paws scratched the cement floor as though she could dig a hole to safety.

"We'll run when the man opens the door," decided Ranger, composing himself.

"That won't work," said Dottie. "He's strong. He'll have Lolly J. on the leash. Let him take her to her crate, and then she can run out with the girl and get away. The girl will be home soon."

"But I need to obey her!" insisted Lolly J.

"Sometimes you just do what you have to do!" Ranger counseled firmly. "Then you fix things up later." He looked out the window.

"Agreed!" shouted Dottie.

"I hate to disappoint her," fretted Lolly J. "But when we come back with Henry, she'll understand."

"That's right. And I'll go with you." Now Dottie was pacing, too.

"If you come, you have to ride in my ear canal," insisted Lolly J. "I don't want you to get hurt."

"Fine."

They watched the man hang his saw and hammer on the wall the way he always did. He put the leash on Lolly J. and opened the door.

"I'm going for it! We can't wait for the girl!" roared Ranger. He lunged at the leash and grabbed it from the man's hand. "Let's go!"

"Awesome!" screamed Dottie as she slid down Lolly J's ear canal.

Ranger ran out of the garage. Lolly J. followed.

"Stop! Stop!" screamed Mr. Rosas. "Come back! I knew you were up to something! I can't chase you! My bad ankle!"

Lolly J. hated disobeying Mr. Rosas. When she and Ranger neared the end of the driveway, the man shouted, "Brian! Brian! The dogs escaped! Help!"

Mr. Macgill ran to the edge of his front yard in time to see the Labrador and the foxhound bolting away like racing dogs. "I can't catch them, Tim!"

"Yee-haw!" Dottie cheered, bouncing in her dark cave. "Ride 'em, cowboy!"

Ranger knew how to watch for cars. When they waited to cross a street, he and Lolly J. scrambled along the curb as passersby tried to grab their collars.

Olivia would have bumped into them while walking home, but her orchestra practice was running late.

The dogs slipped by everyone. In minutes, they had galloped a few blocks past the school to some fields. They ran through the tall grass that rose where city houses stopped and old farmhouses began. Desperate barks streamed out of the second old house they came upon. It was an ancient, neglected house. The roof looked moldy. Wood was missing from the sides. Old tires and eggshells were scattered on the dirt in front.

Ranger and Lolly J. ran to the front door.

"We're here, Dottie!" Lolly J. announced.

"Scratch the door!" Dottie directed, climbing up to the Nine. "Lolly J., howl like a hunter dog. When the woman comes and Ranger runs in, you stay behind him."

"What about Nestor?" asked Lolly J. Her tail jabbed at her stomach.

"Don't worry. I can handle him," vowed Ranger. "And so can you. We'll work together."

"I will do my best," Lolly J. promised. She howled. It wasn't her best howl, but it got someone to the door.

As the dogs and Dottie prepared to enter the house, Olivia was entering her own house. Her grandfather told her the news: her dog was gone.

Tears poured down Olivia's face, but she wiped them with her sleeve. There was no time for emotion.

"Ranger's gone, too," her grandfather reported. "One lucky thing, though: they went west. They went toward the school, so people saw them. Run, Livie, run! Ask everyone. And take your phone."

"I will!" She dropped her violin case and backpack on the floor, put her cell phone in her jacket, zoomed out the door, down the driveway, and headed west.

Olivia talked to everyone she passed. "Two dogs. Did you see two dogs?" She could hardly breathe. "Oh, Daddy!

Daddy! Please let her be okay!" she murmured as she passed the school. "What if she got hit by a car? What if she ran away? What if I never see her again? She's a shy dog; she's trying so hard. Please help! She's in my room at night! She's there in the morning, Daddy!"

"Yes!" said two girls at the playground. They had seen the dogs turn the corner.

"They ran down Oak Street!" said the mailman.

"Past the church!" said the crossing guard.

"Toward the fields!" said the deliveryman.

Propelled by dread, Olivia ran faster than she'd ever run before. When she reached the end of the sidewalk, she plowed through the fields. She heard weak, frantic yelps coming from the house that was falling apart.

She looked around. There was no one in sight. She walked hesitantly up the dirt path. She tried to see into the windows as she approached, but they were covered with saggy curtains. When she reached the house, she grasped the rickety railing and leaned toward the window in the front door. It was too dark inside to see much.

Olivia grabbed her phone, but the door burst open. It was the crazy woman from the pet store with the white cotton-candy hair and red lips! She wore pink pajamas with little crocodiles on them. Olivia put her phone in her pocket.

"Hello, dear," uttered the woman. Her huge grin revealed that some of her lipstick had jumped to her teeth. She ignored a crowd of dogs that were squirming and moaning all around her. "Would you like a cup of tea? You can call me Mildred."

"Hello. My name is Olivia." The girl choked at the smell of the place—old fish and dog poop. She looked beyond the woman into the room. A lopsided chandelier with a couple of small blinking lights cast shadows over seemingly endless eyes roaming in the half-light. They were the eyes of bony dogs, whimpering, whining, and barely able to stand.

"I'm looking for two dogs," said Olivia, reeling on the threshold.

"A Lab and a hound?"

"Right."

"Why, yes! They're visiting, dear! Do come in." Mildred grabbed Olivia's arm and pulled her inside.

CHAPTER 30. LETTING COURAGE OUT

Mildred's red-stained hands pulled Olivia deep into the living room. The floor was a sea of slithering skeletons with fur.

"I'm going to make some gooseberry tea," proclaimed the woman, disappearing behind a tattered sheet hanging in the doorway.

Olivia searched in the dimness for Lolly J. and Ranger. She spotted them both.

Lolly J. stood in a corner next to the baby carriage from the pet store. Her eyes were fixed on a rat-faced black Doberman commanding the center of the room. Ranger sat on the floor near the dog, who was apparently the boss of the place. The Doberman was perched on his throne: a long, dilapidated couch.

Lolly J.'s face lit up when she smelled Olivia's scent. She was so happy to see her girl! She wanted to run to her. But she couldn't leave the carriage.

When Olivia spotted Lolly J., her face lit up, too. She

ran to the carriage. "What are you doing here, Lolly J.?" she whispered. She peered into the carriage. "Is that why you're here? To visit this poor old dog? This place is so gross."

Henry looked up at Olivia. His eyes glistened with terror.

"What's going on here?" Olivia asked.

Lolly J. shot her master an intense look. Then she moved her eyes toward Henry.

"You really are here for this guy. I get it. You are something. I'll try to help."

The Doberman stared hard at Olivia with one eye while he kept the other eye on Ranger. Then he threw his head back, flashed his fangs, and spewed a growl.

Ranger zapped a short, fierce bark at Nestor. The Doberman returned the favor with another killer growl.

"Yikes!" muttered Olivia. "That dog could do some major damage. I don't like Ranger so close."

"That's Nestor, dear," boasted Mildred, popping her head around the sheet. "He keeps things organized. And I think he likes playing with your Lab."

"Playing with the Lab? It looks like he's challenging Ranger to a duel!"

"Oh, fiddlesticks," said the woman before she disappeared behind the sheet again.

The dog room looked as though it had been forgotten since the Declaration of Independence. Layers of wallpaper peeled in a dull rainbow of sooty greens, yellows, and blues. The furniture looked as old as the world. The insides of Nestor's couch hung out like dry cottage cheese. The table near the sheet-door was so warped that someone could lie on the floor and still eat off it. The face of the grandfather clock had lost half its numbers.

A little bony dog collapsed on Olivia's foot. "Whoa!" she exclaimed, and bent down to feel for a pulse in the dog's leg. A distant rhythm beat on her finger. She picked up the black-and-white mutt and placed her hand on his shrunken head.

Lolly J. reached over to lick the dog's cheeks. His eyes opened slightly and focused on the foxhound with a sleepy, pleading stare. Lolly J. then turned her head toward Nestor.

Watching the two invaders attend the bony dog, Nestor barked wildly.

"You hang in there, cutie," Olivia whispered to the little dog. "We'll get help." She put him back on the floor. He went limp.

Olivia ran to the sheet flap. "A dog just keeled over, Mildred!" she shouted through it. "I think he needs water. All these dogs need water. And food."

"Oh, please don't upset our schedule, dear," called the woman's feathery voice. "We have a banquet on Wednesdays and Sundays. You see, all these dogs were homeless when I took them in, except for Henry. They're used to not having much. Nessie's in charge. He gets sardines every day. Baby used to get them, too, but Nestor eats Baby's sardines now. And he likes the cat food left over from the war. He can't stand that Henry's a shelter dog. But don't worry. No one's going to starve around here. Now, let me get our tea."

Olivia flung open the sheet. The woman was standing in what looked like a cave. Centuries of ancient food, probably going back to the Pilgrims, stuck to the walls. The whole cave was lit by one bulb. A mound of broken, reeking dishes lay in the sink. The woman raised a hammer above her head.

Olivia jumped back.

"Don't worry, dear. I'm just squashing our tea." The woman slammed the hammer down into a big, dark-red cluster of berries on a board that looked like it belonged on the side of the house. Her red hands got redder.

"Wonderful," said Olivia. "I can't believe the shelter let you take that dog. I think you need to get organized."

"Oh, they don't know we're in here, honey. I had Henry delivered to my brother's. Elmer lives like a king."

"Wonderful," Olivia said again. She backed through the sheet while Mildred pounded more gooseberries and the blood-colored juice sloshed onto the walls to join the first Thanksgiving dinner.

Lolly J. was now up on her hind legs, her front paws on the edge of the carriage. With her teeth, she was pulling at the straps that were trapping Henry.

"Let me help you!" Olivia ran to the carriage. "I'm just worried about Nestor," she whispered. "He's nuts. He sounds like an elephant." She and Lolly J. stared at the Doberman. He jumped and squirmed. And his howl did sound like an elephant cry. Booming, high, and bossy.

"Ranger, you be careful," cautioned Olivia in a stern voice.

The Lab had started to nip at Nestor's backside. Nestor was not pleased. But he didn't respond. He just stared at Olivia.

Keeping her eyes on Henry's straps, Lolly J. whined with urgency.

"After I undo these, we're getting out!" Olivia quickly unfastened the straps.

Henry jumped out of the carriage and stretched his

shrunken body. His bonnet was big on him now. Slowly he marched his thin, arthritic legs past the bony dogs, toward the front door. Olivia and Lolly J. inched their way behind him.

Nestor kept a beady eye on the three of them. "Where are you going, Baby?" he snarled.

"Take it easy, Nestor," said Ranger coolly, staying close.

"Oh, shut up, you weasel!" Nestor growled.

Henry stopped. He turned toward the Doberman. "When we have visitors, you know she likes me to help out. Don't worry your little head about it, Your Excellency. Save your fish breath."

"You be quiet!" snapped Nestor. "Go back to your bed, or I will devour the Lab and the hound! But I'll get the girl first.

She wants to free my hostage!"

Nestor glowered at Olivia across the room.

The room fell silent. No one moved.

"Holy cow!" cried Dottie from the Nine. "This is like a movie!"

"Who said that? Who said this is like a movie?" *"RAFF! RAFF! RAFF!"* Nestor's high-pitched bark bounced off the walls. "Who am I, Lassie?" He let out a thunderous laugh.

No one answered. When the laugh trailed off, the room fell silent again.

"Do you have friends hiding, Baby?" Nestor bellowed.

Olivia's cell phone rang. It was her mother's ringtone— "Somewhere over the Rainbow" from *The Wizard of Oz*.

"This *is* like a movie!" yelled Dottie as the music soared.

All eyes were on Olivia and the cheery orchestra. She let the call go.

"I've had it! This girl will pay!" growled Nestor. "I'm going for the girl!" He leaped off the couch. Ranger leaped, too, and blocked him. Nestor propelled his head against Ranger's backside and pushed the Lab onto his belly. Then the Doberman raced toward Olivia, but he stumbled on a bony dog. Ranger got up in time to grab Nestor's neck with his teeth.

Olivia scurried to the front door with Lolly J. speeding by her side. Before they could get out, Nestor broke from Ranger's hold and cornered the girl against the door.

Olivia took a deep breath. She stared at the monster, and he stared at her. His eyes were electric. His growl rattled deep in his throat. He flashed his fangs. His legs stiffened. His tail shot up. He was ready to spring.

Lolly J. strode out in front of Olivia and stopped. She pressed her backside against the girl's legs. She stood between Olivia and the Doberman. Her eyes were as electric as his.

"What do I do now?" Lolly J. whispered to Dottie. The foxhound was breathing fast.

"Let your courage out! It's in there!" Dottie whispered back.

Lolly J. stood still. The hair rose on her neck, not in fear but in control. The muscles of her legs tightened to steel. Her tail flipped off her belly and sprang into the air, as high and confident as Nestor's. In a flash, any fear of the Doberman's bloodthirsty face melted away from her. She was no longer his prey. Her head jerked back. Her lips receded. Her fangs shone like shark's teeth. She was ready.

Nestor cocked his head in confusion. Ranger, Henry, and Olivia were mesmerized by the scene before them. Even Mildred, who had popped her head out of the door-sheet, was dumbfounded.

A sound began deep inside the foxhound. It started as almost a purr. It swirled into a juicy, bloodcurdling growl. Then, in an instant, a tsunami roar of a howl shot through her entire being and blasted through the dilapidated walls up to the sky: the unmistakable cry of a savage beast.

CHAPTER 31. A MIGHTY DOT

"Wow!" shrieked Dottie. "Awesome! They can hear you on the moon, Lolly J.!"

"What a wuss!" spewed Nestor. He faced Lolly J. head-on. "You want war? I'll show you war."

Lolly J. stayed calm. She didn't move.

Spittle flew in all directions as the Doberman blathered. "I just can't decide what part of you will be tastiest!" He showed his teeth. Then he lunged toward Lolly J.'s shoulder.

"Watch out! I'm going in!" cried Dottie.

Goo stink hit the air.

Nestor turned away, panting and snorting. "Argh! What is that? I can't take that smell! I can't take it!"

"Let's run for it!" commanded Ranger. "Where's Dottie?"

"Dottie, where are you?" cried Lolly J.

"I have a stink bomb in my nose!" Nestor wailed. Gasping for breath, he galloped around the room.

Lolly J. followed the goo scent straight to Nestor's nose. "Dottie's in Nestor's nose!" she cried. "Dottie, can you hear me?"

No answer.

"Let's get out of here!" ordered Olivia, pulling Lolly J.'s leash.

The foxhound stood firm.

"Dottie will exit on a sneeze," whispered Henry.

"We must catch her," declared Ranger.

"Yes!" Lolly J. held her breath.

Tears spilled from Nestor's eyes. Little puffs of air sputtered from his mouth and erupted into a huge sneeze. A tiny dot shot through the air. Ranger tried to catch it in his mouth, but it moved too fast. It landed in the center of the room near the couch.

Lolly J. ran to sniff it. It was Dottie. She was not moving. There was no time to say anything, no time to check anything. Now that Nestor could breathe, he was ready to attack. Lolly J. licked Dottie up into her mouth. She nodded to Olivia that she was ready. The girl threw open the door and bolted. In an instant, Lolly J. was at her side with Ranger and Henry close behind.

Mildred, holding a cauldron of hot liquid, called from the door. "The tea is finished, Olivia! Come back! Stop! It's Baby's bath night!"

"We have to *go*!" Olivia called back. "I'll give him a bath."

"Oh, thank you, dear!" Mildred put down the tea and waved. "He deserves a vacation."

Olivia and the dogs sped through the fields like a pack until they reached the sidewalk. There was no sign of Nestor, so they stopped to catch their breath.

Olivia called her mother and grandfather, who had been driving around in search of her. "Mission accomplished," she reported. "It's a long story. Lolly J.'s okay. She was very brave. We're on our way. Tell everyone Ranger's a hero."

Ranger introduced himself to Henry and stayed by the old dog as they headed home.

Lolly J. stayed close to Olivia.

"Can we get a taxi?" Henry asked, wheezing hard. "I'm simply not going to make it."

"We'll slow down," said Lolly J. "It's good for you to move."

"You haven't moved much in years," Ranger reminded him.

"I'll try. I will do it for the queen," said Henry.

At a red light, the bulldog's wheezing eased. Olivia slipped off the loose baby bonnet. Henry bowed his head and staggered onward. The pack slowed down to match his pace.

Lolly J. kept her mouth open so that Dottie could get air. The ladybug lay in the middle of the foxhound's tongue. She was still not moving. Lolly J. knew that when a ladybug released goo, it could also play dead when it was really scared. So maybe Dottie was fine. On the other hand, that had been quite a crash on the bare floor. So maybe she wasn't fine. It was horrible not knowing.

At Clover Street, Ranger stopped in front of his house. "I have to be quick. I'm sure my lady is worried. Lolly J., you had so much courage, and you were so calm. I am proud of you."

"Yes, yes! Hear, hear!" toasted Henry, resting on the sidewalk. "I'm immensely grateful to both of you. To Dottie, too, of course. Ranger, your courage was truly exemplary, truly. And you never cease to surprise me, foxhound. From a scaredy-cat to a soldier."

"Thanks, Henry," said Ranger. "I'm glad you're free. Lolly J., let me know about Dottie. Please bark tonight if she's okay."

Lolly J. nodded.

"We'll both bark, we will be so ecstatic," said Henry.

"Good." Ranger sped to the back of his house.

Olivia led Lolly J. and Henry to the Palmers' backyard.

"Poor you," she said, smoothing Henry's fur. "I'll call the shelter to find out about you. And of course I'll give you a bath tomorrow. I promised."

Henry bowed his head. Then he peed under the tree along with Lolly J.

They walked in the back door. No one was home yet. Olivia put out some dog food. Henry gobbled his and slobbered down a large bowl of water. But Lolly J. put nothing in her mouth. She had to keep Dottie as comfortable as possible.

"I know you're a little nervous," Olivia acknowledged.

She ran her hand along her dog's spine. There was a slight quiver to it. "You were so brave today, sweetheart! I can't wait to call Dr. Felder! And Grandma! And Rhett!"

Lolly J.'s eyes were glowing and unafraid. She looked at her master with fervent dedication.

"Oh, my, Lolly J.! You have so much feeling!" Olivia kissed Lolly J.'s head spot. "I hope you don't mind if Henry stays in our room tonight. Maybe you knew him at the shelter."

The dog wanted to lick Olivia, but she couldn't with the guest in her mouth.

Olivia left the room.

Henry looked around. "This is a nice, orderly house, foxhound. You're very lucky. Not a lot of fools running around. And the girl is spectacular."

Olivia came back with an old, folded-up crate. She wiped off the cobwebs. "It's from before I was born. But it will do." She carted it up the stairs with the dogs scampering behind. Then she set up the crate and laid down a soft yellow blanket from her bed. "Okay, guys. I'll keep your doors open so you can visit if you want. I just know you're buddies."

She moved the books from her desk to her dresser. Voices came up from downstairs. She closed the door and left to tell her story.

CHAPTER 32. SOME THINGS LAST FOREVER

"Okay, foxhound, let out the bug," directed Henry as he left his crate and joined Lolly J.

Lolly J. bent down and shook her tongue gently over her blanket. Dottie rolled out easily.

"She likes to be called an insect," Lolly J. reminded Henry.

"I'm sorry."

Lolly J. and Henry studied Dottie. Her stink had receded. She didn't move.

"Oh, Dottie. You look so dried up! Are you okay?" Lolly J. put her snout down next to the ladybug. Still no movement. "Do your wings hurt? What can I do for you?"

Henry looked at Dottie's motionless body. He put his paw down on Lolly J.'s. "I'm afraid she's gone."

"No, she's not, Henry. Are your eyes that bad? Can't you see her? She's right here." Lolly J. yanked her paw away from Henry's and sat up.

"I mean, I think she's dead."

"Really?" Lolly J.'s eyes were watery and wide.

"Right."

"Forever?"

"Right." Henry had tears, too. He bowed his head.

"I guess we won't be sending Ranger any barks," lamented Lolly J.

"No." Henry shook his head.

Lolly J. inched her nose toward Dottie until it was touching her tiny, brittle body. Tears ran down onto the ladybug. "I told Ranger I'd try," said the foxhound, "but I still don't think I can live without you, Dottie."

"I told you I would stay until you had your human," came Dottie's voice, thin and faraway.

"But I want both of you!"

Dottie's underwater voice sounded again. "Well, you can have us both."

"Really? Where are you?"

"I'm inside you."

"You are?"

"Yes, I'm a memory now. You can still love me. I can still love you. We can even talk."

"Just like before!" Lolly J. stood up and wagged her tail. "Oh, Dottie, I'm wagging my tail! My tail is wagging!"

"Wonderful!" squealed Dottie. "This is fantastic. You are a true, whole dog!"

"I am!" Lolly J.'s tail swished with joy.

"But I must tell you that it will not be exactly like before. Memories are not like life. I am no longer in your life." Dottie's voice flowed like dream talk. "Part of you will feel empty," she said. "You will miss me. But memories help fill emptiness. The rest you fill in yourself."

"But I have no life without you."

"Yes you do, foxhound. You have your human, your girl! And the smell of the earth and the snow that's coming soon and the man in the garage . . . and adventures every day that you don't even know about yet. And you have Ranger. And even Henry now."

"And all the ladybugs in hibernation," added Lolly J.

"Yes, hundreds of them! That is your life!"

"But you are my biggest, most wonderful memory!" The foxhound danced around the room. Her tail wagged with a life of its own now.

"Is she talking to you, foxhound?" asked Henry. "Your tail is brilliant, I say."

"Yes, she is, she is! Dottie is inside me!"

"That's how it works." Exhausted, Henry sat on his new blanket. He looked at Dottie. "We must do something with what's left of her. What shall we do?"

"We could take her to the spa," suggested Lolly J.

"The old girl had a spa?"

"Yes, Hibernation Spa."

"I say, doesn't sound quite like the right final resting place."

Lolly J. looked around. "We could put her in the plant by the window. It's the nearest thing to a shrub. And she loves shrubs."

They both looked over at the leafy plant in a large bowl.

"Perfect," agreed Henry.

Lolly J. leaned over. "I am going to put you in a safe place, my friend." She licked the ladybug up from the blanket and carried her to the plant. She rolled Dottie gently onto the soil and made a small hole with her paw. Then, with great care, she placed the ladybug into the hole.

Henry walked over to inspect. "You need to cover her up, foxhound."

"Why? I want to keep track of her."

"Nature likes earth on top," Henry said. "Bodies don't last forever. They become part of the earth."

"I see." It was almost too much to imagine Dottie disappearing. But with the memory inside her, Lolly J. moved soil over the ladybug. "Good-bye, Dottie. Ciao, bambina." She patted it down with her paw. For the longest time, Lolly J. sat by the plant. Her tail stopped wagging.

Henry sat next to her.

Then a strange thing happened at the window. Little white specks started falling. They didn't sound like rain. They didn't have a sound at all.

"That's snow," said Henry.

"Oh, my." Lolly J. watched the flakes, magnificent and silent, dance behind the plant as dusk turned to night.

CHAPTER 33. FILLING THE NINE

When Olivia returned to her room, she found the dogs sitting quietly at the window.

"Time for our last walk," she announced. She put a leash on each of them. "Mom called Lynn. Of course you guys are buddies. I knew that was what all the fuss was about."

The dogs didn't understand a word. But they knew Olivia was serious, and they knew she was in charge.

"Henry's going to live with Mr. Macgill right next door," she told them. "And all those bony dogs, they're going to the shelter—tonight! The lady in the old house, her name is Mrs. Flonce. She's happy with just Nestor. But she gets to visit Henry once a month. Mr. Macgill's okay with it."

Lolly J. and Henry raced down the stairs with the happy, decisive girl. Lolly J. dashed into the thin layer of snow and plunged her nose into it. She loved the cold powder under her paws. She pranced in circles.

The two dogs peed under the tree. Then Henry went to check the perimeter.

Lolly J. stood still to let the snow collect on her back. She wagged her tail.

"Wow!" cheered Olivia. "Lolly J., your tail is moving! What a happy tail! What an afternoon! What is happening to you?" She sat down on the bench near the tree and gazed at her remarkable dog. Lolly J. walked up to the girl just as she had at the shelter months earlier. She nestled her snout on Olivia's knees. She wasn't trembling this time. Neither was the girl.

Olivia stroked Lolly J.'s head spot. She leaned down to whisper in the dog's ear, across the Nine that was empty now. "I love you!" Olivia dropped her hand to Lolly J.'s tummy, which was empty now, too, without the tail against it. She scratched her dog softly. Lolly J. purred. "I'll show you how to cross the street just in case you have another mission," Olivia said. "But you better not!"

Lolly J. lifted her head and looked into Olivia's eyes. Olivia was her universe now. She loved the way the girl rubbed her tummy. The comfort was almost overwhelming. She licked the girl's cheek.

Olivia felt the warm tongue on her face. The comfort was almost overwhelming.

She hugged Lolly J. ever so gently. The dog and her girl, the girl and her dog, stayed together without a word, the snow falling onto them as one.

"I think you love me, Lolly J.," whispered Olivia. Her tears dropped onto the dog's snout. She knelt at Lolly J.'s side. "You know what? The thing is, I needed taming, too."

Lolly J. licked the girl's tears. They tasted better than anything in all the world.

They returned to the bedroom with Henry. The bulldog went right to sleep in his crate. But Lolly J. couldn't take her eyes off the girl. She watched Olivia fall asleep while reading her book. She watched the book drop to the floor.

Dottie had said Lolly J. would know when to go to Olivia's

bed. It was time. The foxhound got up and walked across the room. She placed her front paws on the edge of the mattress and jumped up. Inch by inch, she crawled to the girl. She sniffed Olivia's arm, stretched out on the covers. She passed her nose ever so lightly along her fingers, her wrist, and up to her elbow. She breathed the girl's scent deeply and then landed in a cuddle at her feet.

"This is where you belong," murmured Dottie.

Olivia opened her eyes. She sat up. She gazed at her dog with wonder. She bent down and kissed Lolly J.'s snout. "This is where you belong," she murmured.

Lolly J. slid up toward the girl. They both exhaled as though until this moment they hadn't quite breathed right. Then they sank into the bed.

Olivia curled up on her side under the covers. Lolly J. rested her head on the warm, round ledge of the girl's hip. Her tail rose and softly wagged in celebration as the scents of Dottie and Olivia mingled in the air.

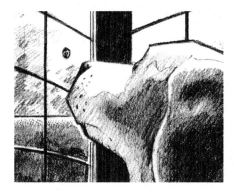

ACKNOWLEDGEMENTS

A heartfelt thank-you to the awesome crew that gathered around as this project picked up steam.

Noah Webster MicroSociety Magnet School principals Dee Cole and Jay Mihalko offered steady encouragement as Tess and I roamed their halls through the years. They gamely accepted the rock-star commotion that greeted Tess's visits.

Fifth-grade teacher, Kelly Cykley, was unflappable and supportive as Tess and I gradually became fixtures in her classroom, where I had the treat of watching three crops of students evolve into impressive readers—direct, substantial, and confident in their observations.

Linda Ostiguy, a wise veterinary technician and friend of Tess's; Stoddard Lane-Reticker, Tess's trainer, who pitched in the very first week; and Dr. Steve Feldman, Tess's vet, all shared their insights into the most removed-from-reality dog they had ever met.

Marilyn Douglas, the best friend of the real-life yellow Lab, Ranger—a therapy dog who befriended and tutored Tess early on—helped me understand the special connection between the two dogs.

Shannon Keith, founder and president of the Beagle Freedom Project and Animal Rescue Media Education (ARME), increased my awareness of the many issues and details embedded in the rescue and rehabilitation of dogs like Tess, who have been cut off from the world and are familiar only with a warehouse drudge routine.

Dr. David Grisé, pulmonologist extraordinaire (for humans) and nature's gift to Airedales, orchestrated with warmth and optimism my victory over a protracted lung challenge in the middle of working on this book.

At the outset of the writing process, I turned to four friends who are well acquainted with the realm of children's literature: Susan Aller, Louise Blalock, Mims Butterworth, and Martha Rosenthal. I am grateful for their frank responses to my first manuscript and to my ambitious intentions. They let me know that I had a long road ahead, and I decided to travel it.

My next round of early readers was an intrepid lot willing to enter a world of talking animals and insects while staying grounded enough to respond to larger themes. Many thanks to this dedicated crew: Mary Chamberlain, Heather Clifford, Kelly Cykley, Marilyn Douglas, Linda Ostiguy, Nancy Rankin, Annelieke Schauer, and Jane Torrey. In addition, drafts were read by Sean Clifford, Iris Febles-Martinez, Ethel Fried, Deb Hellman, Joan Scott, Margaret Sleezer, Cynthia Sugerman, and Caroline White.

Stacy DeKeyser gave a helpful early manuscript evaluation. My editor, Nikki Bruno Clapper, provided an invaluable no-nonsense and patiently iterative scouring.

Artist Matt Ryan, who warned me that illustrating a pea-size costar was near folly, managed in the end to depict the impossibly challenging Dottie, as well as the rest of the book's characters, in the simple, classic way I desired, with a fresh, contemporary twist.

Tess's and my partner in life, Ken, galvanized this entire project. He insisted that my musings be put to paper and then endured every permutation of the chaos that followed.

Of course, above all, I salute Tess. When she was introduced to the world, experts thought her protective state of shock would last forever. How wrong they were!

As I was completing the manuscript, Tess died unexpectedly. She was fourteen and a half. At that ripe old age, she was a kind, gracious, brave dog. She had also developed a sly sense of humor. But that's for another book.

Photographs by Léa Girard

ABOUT THE PUBLISHER

Bradley Street Press publishes exceptional books that embody classic themes with a contemporary twist.

info@bradleystreetpress.com

ABOUT THE AUTHOR

Martha Ritter wrote her first book when she was in the sixth grade. It was a huge volume about the Republic of Indonesia, which the president of the United States requested she give to Indonesia's president. Reluctantly, she complied—and nearly caused an international incident.

Despite this complication, Ms. Ritter has been writing ever since. A journalist, speechwriter, and poet, she has served as a public affairs director for the City of New York.

As a New York actor, Ms. Ritter has worked in theater and shared her sense of humor with a national audience in a number of classic TV commercials. This is her first children's book.

Ms. Ritter lives in Connecticut and New York City.

ABOUT THE ILLUSTRATOR

Matt Ryan is an illustrator, cartoonist, and arts educator. He is the artist for Connecticut's Free Lunch Comics and also creates artwork for a variety of industries.

The Comicbook Artists Guild recognized Mr. Ryan with its best cartoonist award and its first-ever award for production excellence at the New York Comic Con. He has headed Connecticut's branch of the Comicbook Artists Guild and the Granby Artists Association.

Mr. Ryan has served as a member of the faculty of the Farmington Valley Arts Center in Farmington, Connecticut. Named a Master Teaching Artist by the Greater Hartford Arts Council, he teaches drawing at a number of schools around the state.

Mr. Ryan lives in Connecticut with his wife and two daughters.

CPSIA information can be obtained at www.ICGtesting.com
Printed in the USA
BVOW08s0327110515

399526BV00002B/2/P

9 780986 381713